DISCOVER MEDIEVAL SANDWICH

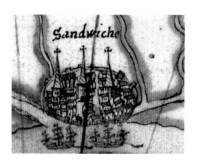

Discover Medieval Sandwich

A GUIDE TO ITS HISTORY AND BUILDINGS

Helen Clarke

Oxbow Books
Oxford and Oakville

Published by
Oxbow Books, Oxford, UK

ISBN 978-1-84217-476-0

This book is available direct from

Oxbow Books, Oxford, UK
(Phone: 01865-241249; Fax: 01865-794449)

and

The David Brown Book Company
PO Box 511, Oakville, CT 06779, USA
(Phone: 860-945-9329; Fax: 860-945-9468)

or from our website

www.oxbowbooks.com

A CIP record for this book is available from the British Library

Printed in Great Britain by
Information Press, Eynsham, Oxfordshire

Contents

Acknowledgements

This work is one of the outcomes of the Sandwich Project, supported by English Heritage from 2004 to 2008. One of the aims of the project was to publish an academic study of Sandwich; this appeared in 2010 as *Sandwich: The 'completest medieval town in England'*, by Helen Clarke, Sarah Pearson, Mavis Mate and Keith Parfitt. Another of the project's aims was to present the town to the general reader in a well-illustrated book with a short text, written by one of the project's participants and based on its findings. The author is very grateful to English Heritage, and especially Colum Giles, for their support and for allowing the reproduction of many photographs specially taken for the project.

Thanks are also due to many others for their help and encouragement. John Hills of Canterbury Christ Church University drew the maps. Allan Adams and Howard Jones are responsible for the line-drawings. Jeremy Tafler took some of the photographs, and Ray Harlow of the Sandwich Guildhall Archive provided others. Tracey Ward, Sandwich Town Clerk, has been an unfailing source of information. A number of experts read the text in draft, and I thank them all. Foremost must be Sarah Pearson, a friend and colleague from the Sandwich Project, but I am also very grateful to Birte Brugmann, Meriel Connor, Lesley Orson and Jayne Semple for their helpful suggestions. I have also had fruitful discussions with Val Lamb who is responsible for the design, and with Clare Litt who saw the book through the press. But by far the biggest thank-you goes to Giles, my long-suffering husband, who has acted as chauffeur, photographer and grammarian with unstinting patience.

All the above have helped to make this book what it is, but I remain responsible for the final outcome and any mistakes that may have crept in.

Helen Clarke
Tunbridge Wells, August 2011

Attributions for the illustrations are given as follows:

ATA	Allan Adams	HJ	Howard Jones
BC	Barry Corke	JH	John Hills
BOYS	W. Boys, *Collections for an History of Sandwich in Kent*, 1792	JT	Jeremy Tafler
		KP	Keith Parfitt
CAT	Canterbury Archaeological Trust	RH	Ray Harlow
EH NMR	English Heritage National Monuments Record	ROLFE	H. W. Rolfe, *The Publications of the Antiquarian Etching Club*, 1852
GC	Giles Clarke	SGA	Sandwich Guildhall Archive
HC	Helen Clarke		

Foreword

The beautiful town of Sandwich has more to it than meets the eye. With its three ancient churches and its many early timber-framed houses, the place is obviously one of great antiquity, but at a superficial glance it might be mistaken for a typical Kentish market town on the bank of the lazy river Stour. What is not apparent today is that in the medieval period Sandwich was one of England's most important seaports. The Stour is a vestigial reminder of a maritime heritage, being the shrunken relic of Sandwich Haven, once the anchorage for great fleets, both commercial and military.

The history of the town has been the subject of a long-term collaborative project which brought together experts from many disciplines looking at documents, topography, archaeology and buildings. The full results of the research project have been published in an academic monograph, which establishes Sandwich's significance in a national context. The story is too interesting and important to be confined to a specialist academic audience, however, and Helen Clarke has succeeded in the present book in making the research available in an attractive, accessible and affordable form to a much broader constituency.

English Heritage has supported the research project on Sandwich and welcomes the publication of this book. It fulfils many of our core objectives, but most especially it will lead to increased understanding and enjoyment of the town's history and historic environment. Through enjoyment will come better care, and if we care we will protect those places which we value as significant.

Colum Giles
English Heritage

Timeline 1

Sandwich		General	Reigns	
St Wilfrid to Sandwich Haven	*c.*665		664–73	Ecgberht I of Kent
Nine Viking ships destroyed in the Haven	851	Vikings stayed over winter in Thanet	839–58	Aethelwulf & Aethelstan I
Norwegian Viking fleet in the Haven	993	Vikings attacked E. Anglia	978–1016	Aethelred II
St Clement's built in stone	*c.*1000			
Danish Viking fleet in the Haven	1006			
Anglo-Saxon Viking fleet in the Haven	1009	Continual Viking attacks		
Canute visited Sandwich as Viking raider	1014			
King Canute issued charter to Christ Church Priory	1023	England & Denmark united	1016–35	Canute the Great
King Harthacanute in Sandwich	1039		1035–42	Harthacanute
King Edward at Sandwich with Anglo-Saxon fleet	1044, 1049, 1050, 1052	More Viking attacks	1042–66	Edward Confessor
St Peter's built in stone	*c.*1050			
	1066		1066	Harold Godwinson
	1066	Battle of Hastings	1066–87	William I
Sandwich then with 383 dwellings	1086	Domesday Book		
St Mary's built	*c.*1100		1087–1100	William II
Delf diverted to town	*c.*1100		1100–35	Henry I
St Clement's tower built	1100s			
Urban privileges granted by Henry I	1120s			
			1135–54	Stephen
	1152	Duchy of Aquitaine acquired as dowry		
Urban privileges confirmed by Henry II	1150s		1154–89	Henry II
Thomas Becket disembarks in Haven	1170			
	1189	Cinque Port privileges		
Sandwich's first mayor	by 1200		1189–99	Richard I

Developments in Sandwich *c.*665–*c.*1200 set against major events in the history of England

1 The Formative Years

Introduction

Today Sandwich in Kent is a town of about 5,000 inhabitants, standing on the river Stour and about 3km inland from the English Channel. Its narrow, twisting streets lined by historic houses are a visible reminder of the Middle Ages, a time when Sandwich was one of the most important ports in England. Then, its harbour provided a safe haven for royal fleets that assembled there before setting out on warlike expeditions, and it was also the destination for cargo ships from European ports, especially those carrying luxuries such as wine, spices and silks from the Mediterranean. The merchants dealing in these goods built themselves impressive timber-framed houses, many of which are still lived in today and which give the town its unique character – a busy 21st-century town, but clearly rooted in its medieval past.

The changing landscape: Sandwich Haven and its rivers

The single geographical feature that made Sandwich different from most other towns in medieval England was its harbour, the Haven, which transformed a settlement serving the surrounding countryside into a port with royal and international connections. The importance of Sandwich Haven may not be immediately apparent today as the name is applied to the couple of kilometres of meandering river Stour flowing from the bridge in the middle of Sandwich to the south-west corner of Pegwell Bay. It is difficult to imagine this as an international port, and of course it could never have been so in its present form. It was once very different, as can be seen in Figure 1.1 which shows the area around Sandwich a thousand or so years ago. The Haven then was a calm anchorage to the west of a shingle spit ('Pepperness' on Figure 1.1 but now know as the Deal or Sandwich Bay Spit) which protected it from the rough waters of the English Channel. This in

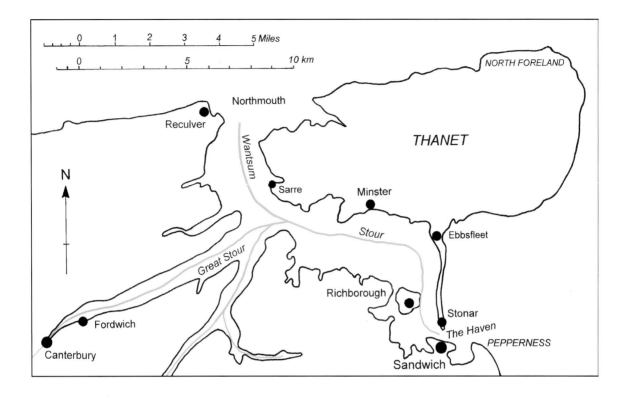

itself would have encouraged the growth of a port on its bank, but it had the added advantage of being at the south-eastern end of a navigable waterway from the Outer Thames Estuary to the English Channel. This consisted of the rivers Stour and Wantsum which, with their flood plains, became known as the Wantsum Channel. In the Middle Ages the route was much used by ships sailing to and from London and the ports of the east coast of England. By using the Wantsum Channel they could avoid the notoriously dangerous sea passage around the North Foreland.

Sandwich Haven first became known as the place where fleets of warships could gather together in safety during the years of conflict between Anglo-Saxon England and Viking Scandinavia in the 9th and 10th centuries, but in later years it was visited by more peaceful vessels. And so the port town grew and prospered through its waterborne contacts until a combination of human intervention and natural phenomena clogged up the lifeblood of the town.

Figure 1.1 Sandwich Haven at the south-east end of the waterways through the Wantsum Channel. 'Pepperness' is the medieval name for the north point of the Deal Spit, which sheltered the Haven during most of the Middle Ages
(HC/BC)

As the rivers and 'Pepperness' have changed over the centuries, so has the countryside around Sandwich, much of which lies in the flood plains and is nowhere more than 4m above sea level (Figure 1.2). Now dry and fertile, it once was marshy land of no agricultural value and probably regarded as useless waste. A lot of it belonged to monasteries, such as those at Reculver and Minster-in-Thanet, which had been founded in the early years of English Christianity (the 7th and 8th centuries) by monks from the religious centre of Canterbury. It came into their possession because kings, aristocrats or other great landowners gave it to the monasteries in exchange for the monks' prayers, which they hoped would save their souls. This was a common practice in the Middle Ages, but often what was given was poor

Figure 1.2 Aerial view of Sandwich from the south-west showing drained and reclaimed land between the town and the sea, which can be glimpsed in the background
(EH NMR 24064/04)

quality land on the margins of the lordly estates which was unproductive and difficult to cultivate. But sometimes the land had great potential, as can be seen in Yorkshire, for example, where the Cistercian monks of Fountains Abbey transformed scrubland into highly profitable sheep runs. The wetlands around the Wantsum and Stour had similar potential. Once drained, they became fertile arable fields or lush pasture where the monks could raise animals. Other landlords in the Wantsum Channel then followed the monks' example by draining and improving their property, so that marsh was gradually replaced by fields, and the landscape became the one we know today.

Although they did not realize it at the time, by beginning the process of draining the marshland and flood plains the medieval landowners had been doing a great service to the inhabitants of modern Sandwich. The wet and swampy areas were ideal breeding grounds for mosquitoes, and therefore for malaria, known as 'ague' in the Middle Ages and 'marsh fever' more recently. This was as much of a scourge of the Sandwich population as the frequent recurrences of the plague, for although it was not immediately fatal it lowered resistance to other illnesses. It was not until the 19th century that the land around Sandwich was sufficiently dry for the disease to die out.

But as we shall see, draining the land also did a great disservice to the town as it helped to change the course of the rivers, and eventually to ruin Sandwich's economy. Some landowners constructed weirs across the rivers to improve the fishing on their stretch. Others erected watermills to grind the grain grown in their newly reclaimed fields; this involved digging millponds whose dams also obstructed the rivers. Finally, in the 1600s, the Northern Sea Wall was built between Reculver and Birchington to protect the reclaimed lands of the Wantsum Channel from the sea (Figure 1.3). The river Wantsum was blocked and diverted so that it no longer flowed into the Thames estuary to provide a short cut for shipping. The river Stour became the only navigable waterway.

The landscape and waterways have been radically changed by human intervention, but nature has also played its part. The sluggish rivers have always deposited the silt that they pick up in their upper reaches, forming shoals and sandbanks which divert the currents and make the waters shallower, but by far the greatest change was caused by the growth of the Deal Spit. This was a barrier between the river and the English Channel

Figure 1.3 The Northern Sea Wall blocking the mouth of the river Wantsum. Birchington on the Isle of Thanet can be seen in the background

(HC)

formed by longshore drift. In this process, which is still continuing, the tides, waves and winds carry sand and shingle northwards along the coast from further south, and then deposit them on the sea shore to the north and east of Sandwich (Figure 1.4). Until the 1400s this was an advantage to the town, for the spit sheltered the Stour estuary from the rough seas of the English Channel and provided a calm anchorage for all sorts of ships, from the greatest merchantmen that England, Italy or France could build, to royal fleets preparing for war.

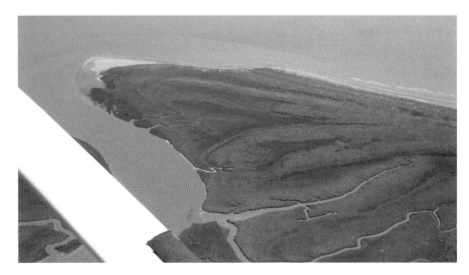

Figure 1.4 Aerial view of the north end of the Deal Spit, now called Shell Ness. The shingle ridges deposited by longshore drift are clearly visible although now mostly covered in grass

(CAT F11845_6203)

About a thousand years ago the spit was very much shorter than it is today, its north end (medieval Pepperness, now called Shell Ness) being represented by one of the shingle ridges which have built up over time. The geological map on Figure 1.5 shows the sand and shingle ridges which form the spit, with the ridge just north of New Downs Farm and Broad Salts probably representing the Pepperness of *c.*1000 when it was about 5km south of the southern shore of the Isle of Thanet. Nowadays Shell Ness is only 2km south of Thanet and the longshore drift that started the process is still moving the point of the spit northwards at a rate of about 2m every year. If it continues at this rate, in about 500 years it will stretch right across Pegwell Bay, as far as the Isle of Thanet itself.

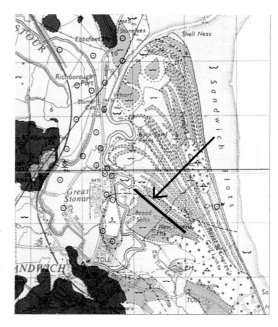

Figure 1.5 The probable northern extremity of the Deal Spit in the Early Middle Ages is represented by a shingle ridge just north of Broad Salts and New Downs Farm, indicated by the arrow

Sandwich's beginnings

The history of Sandwich begins long before there was a prosperous town inhabited by wealthy merchants. The first historical reference to the name can be found in a manuscript entitled the *Life of St Wilfrid*, written in the early 8th century. It includes an anecdote about Wilfrid's voyage from the coast of France to York in the year 665. After various adventures Wilfrid's ship sighted a landmark that the author calls *Sandwic*, perhaps the south bank of Sandwich Haven where it could drop anchor in calm water in the lee of the Deal Spit (see Figure. 1.1). There is no suggestion that Wilfrid set foot on dry land, nor that there was any sort of settlement there at the time. The importance of *Sandwic* was in its anchorage and its position at the beginning of the route through the Wantsum Channel along which Wilfrid could have sailed. After reaching Northmouth his ship would have crossed the Outer Thames Estuary to continue its journey up the east coast of England to the Humber, and then along the river Ouse to York where he was to become bishop.

There is no evidence for a town at Sandwich until about the year 1000 when St Clement's, the first of its churches, was built in stone. It stood on

Figure 1.6 Aerial view
of St Clement's church
which was a prominent
landmark, overlooking
the now silted harbour

(EH NMR 24064/06)

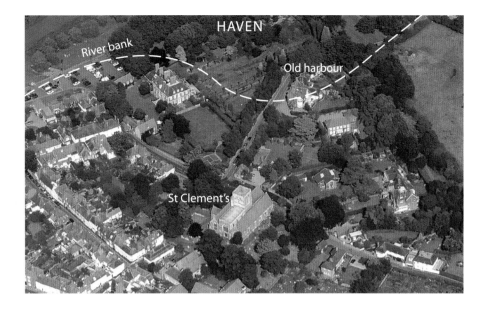

a relatively high point in the low-lying land, overlooking the Haven (Figure 1.6), and formed the nucleus of a little settlement which was to grow into the town. A couple of decades later Christ Church Priory in Canterbury founded a small administrative centre, like a manor house, on a knoll of dry land only 500m west of St Clement's (see page 8). These two sites came to mark the eastern and western limits of the town which grew up between them.

The earliest town: the 11th century

We can have only a hazy picture of the town and the people who lived in it in its first few decades, but there are some clues. When St Clement's church was built, there were probably people living in the neighbourhood who could form the core of the congregation. They may have made their living largely from the sea, as fishermen or even by providing victualling services for the fleets of Anglo-Saxon warships which anchored in Sandwich Haven in the decades around 1000. Once Canute the Great became king of both England and Denmark in 1016, the Haven may have changed its role, becoming a convenient landing place for travellers from the Continent, including visiting royalty. Canute's queen, Emma, must have sailed into the

Haven at least once on her way to or from Denmark, for in her biography Sandwich is described as one of the 'most renowned of all the ports of the English'. Perhaps it was because of Emma's good opinion that in 1023 King Canute gave Christ Church Priory the right to charge tolls on ships sailing through the Wantsum Channel and also to run, and charge for, the ferry which plied between Sandwich and Stonar, then a small settlement on the other bank.

King Canute also granted the monks the revenues in cash and kind (herrings) from the developing port of Sandwich. Christ Church Priory greatly benefited from these concessions, and the little secular settlement near St Clement's may also have experienced change. As far as the Priory was concerned, the money from the tolls must have led to a financial bureaucracy, and the equivalent of a modern estate office was set up at the western edge of what was to become the medieval town, conveniently placed at the east end of the Ash causeway, along which monks and officials could travel to and from their Canterbury headquarters. The tolls directly benefited the Priory, but others might have profited more indirectly. Merchantmen wanting to sail through the Wantsum Channel probably had to drop anchor in the Haven while waiting to pay their tolls, and the locals could have taken advantage of this by rowing out with fresh food, water and other goods to sell to the sailors. The economy and the population must have been on an upward curve.

When Edward the Confessor reasserted Anglo-Saxon sovereignty in 1042 warships again used Sandwich Haven as an anchorage, assembling there against potential Viking attacks. The king himself visited his fleets at least four times, and on one of his visits he attended mass at St Clement's church. This was a great honour for the church, but also for the developing town which was growing extraordinarily quickly. By 1086 Sandwich was the third largest town in Kent after Canterbury and Dover. Domesday Book records that in the time of King Edward there had been 307 habitable houses in Sandwich (so about 1,500 people), but that by 1086 there were 383 dwellings (for about 2,000 inhabitants).

The network of streets along which the houses clustered was much the same as today. The street pattern developed on this area because of the underlying geology of Sandwich which had an enormous influence throughout history. The settlement stands on a low ridge of sandy clay, known as Thanet Beds, which is surrounded on three sides by alluvial deposits which, in contrast to the dry sandy clay, were once wet and marshy. When Sandwich was first settled in the early 11th century the marshland was too wet to be built on, so streets and houses were confined to the dry land on the ridge. The ridge is not much more than 7m above sea level at its topmost point, and to the casual eye the town seems to stand on totally flat land. But that is not so, even if the changes in contours are very slight. St Clement's church, for example, stands on ground that is noticeably higher than Market Street (on the edge of the Thanet Beds at *c.*3.5m above sea level) or the site of the Guildhall in the Cattle Market (on Alluvium *c.*2m above sea level).

The areas of Alluvium were drained by ditches which carried water into a system of dykes, ditches and sluices which led it away from the town. This eventually dried out the land sufficiently for the friary to be built on it at the end of the 13th century. Two of the dykes are now known as The Rope walk and the Butts, which became part of the town defences in the 14th century.

Figures 1.7A–1.7C (overleaf) show the medieval streets of Sandwich and how the geology that underlies them has dictated their line. Those on the higher ground were laid out in the earliest years and many of them were continuations of roads from the countryside, some leading down to the ferry across the river Stour to Stonar and the Isle of Thanet. The main road from Canterbury came in from the west to reach the Priory's outstation, roughly where Old Manwood School is shown on the map. At that time it was no more than a track, and beyond St Mary's church the Strand Street that we know today only came into existence after the riverside land had been drained and consolidated. The first houses, built no earlier than *c.*1300, were well south of the south bank of the river (see page 42). The aerial view on Figure 1.8 shows the sinuous line of Strand Street, reflecting the probable bank of the river before the reclamation took place.

There are fewer streets on the drained land, and they cannot have been in place until the 1350s. One of them is New Street (meaning that it was new in the Middle Ages). Its continuation is Delf Street; another interesting street name for it is on the bank of the Delf stream, a watercourse that closely follows the edge of the higher land.

The only remains that we have from the buildings in the town at this time are a few stones in the churches, but they can be used to reconstruct what

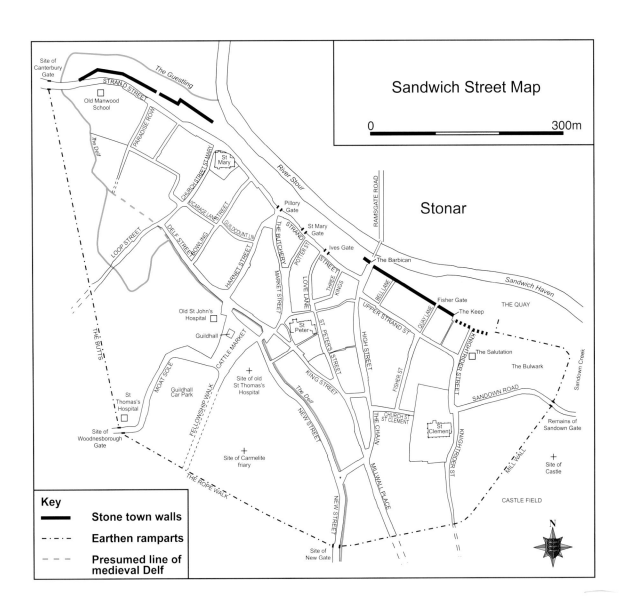

Sandwich Street Map

0 _____ 300m

Stonar

Key

━━━━━ Stone town walls

─ · ─ · ─ Earthen ramparts

─ ─ ─ ─ Presumed line of medieval Delf

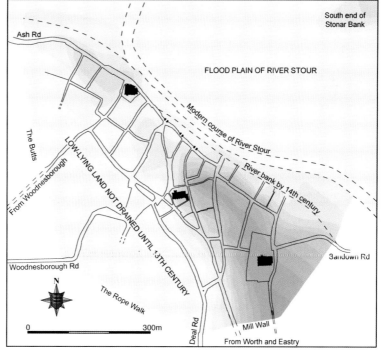

Figure 1.8 The eastern half of Strand Street marks the position of the bank of the river Stour before the 14th century; the straighter western section was modified in the 18th century

(EH NRM 24073/20)

N

Strand Street

St Mary's

the churches looked like in the 11th century (Figure 1.9). St Clement's may appear a simple building in this drawing, but in reality it must have seemed very grand indeed to people who lived out their lives in small, single-storeyed, dark, smoky, wooden huts. Churches would have dominated every urban landscape, being many times larger than any other building in a town. They were designed for the glory of God and so great resources were lavished on them and they were built to the highest standards of their time, and often elaborately furnished with wall hangings and crucifixes. We know that when King Edward chose St Clement's as a suitable place to attend

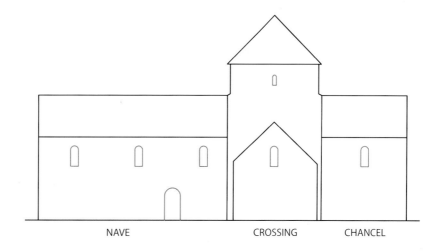

Figure 1.9 Reconstruction of St Clement's church in the 11th century
(HJ/ATA)

NAVE   CROSSING   CHANCEL

divine service, its interior was decorated with a fine woven wall-hanging behind the altar and a crucifix above it. It must have been the most imposing church in Sandwich in the middle of the 11th century. Some stones that survive in St Peter's church indicate that it was built in the 11th century, but sometime later than St Clement's. Too little is left of it for a reconstruction to be attempted, and the same is true of the third parish church, St Mary's, probably founded at the turn of the 11th and 12th centuries.

Although none of the houses mentioned in Domesday Book survives, we can still get a feel for the town as it was then by looking at the modern streets. They are now covered in tarmac, and have kerbstones and pavements, whereas originally they would have been dusty, or muddy, tracks along the Thanet Beds ridge, leading from the countryside to the riverbank. But although their appearance may differ today, their layout is the same as it has ever been. Imagine the modern streets lined with single-storey wooden houses, each in a yard surrounded by a wooden fence. Hens and pigs may have been roaming around, poking about in the rubbish, and there may have been a privy, but there was almost certainly no well or other source of water. Until the Delf was canalized and diverted through the town, water would have had to be brought from the river.

It was a hard life for the fishermen, mariners, artisans and labourers who lived in 11th-century Sandwich, although some rich families might have enjoyed a better standard of living. These may have filled the roles of leaders of a society which, although simple, had to meet certain obligations. Some people would have come to the fore in arranging the collection of taxes in kind or the organization of the fishing fleet and a bureaucracy of some sort emerged. Unfortunately we know nothing about who led the people of Sandwich in the 11th century, but the obligations to the Priory and Crown suggest that they were involved with fishing or seafaring.

There were two main obligations that the townspeople had to meet every year. The Priory demanded 40,000 herrings annually, and the Crown demanded 'ship service'. In the case of Sandwich, that meant providing the king with 20 ships for fifteen days each year and for each ship a crew of 21 men. Sandwich was one of five ports in the South East that had to perform this duty. The four others were the Kentish ports of Dover, Hythe and New Romney, and Hastings in Sussex. Together they became known as the Cinque Ports, a loose association of ports with similar obligations but with a certain amount of independence. The king attempted to assert his authority over them by appointing a Lord Warden of the Cinque Ports, resident in Dover Castle. This office was already established by 1226, and there is still a Lord Warden today, although it is now an honorary title and the residence is the 16th-century Walmer Castle. It was not until 1260 that a royal charter gave the group of ports a formal status, and by then it was seven strong because Rye and Winchelsea had joined. But the charter referred to the Cinque (Five) Ports, and that name has been applied to all seven ever since. Rye and Winchelsea were often called the 'ancient towns' as they were not part of the original group (Figure 1.10).

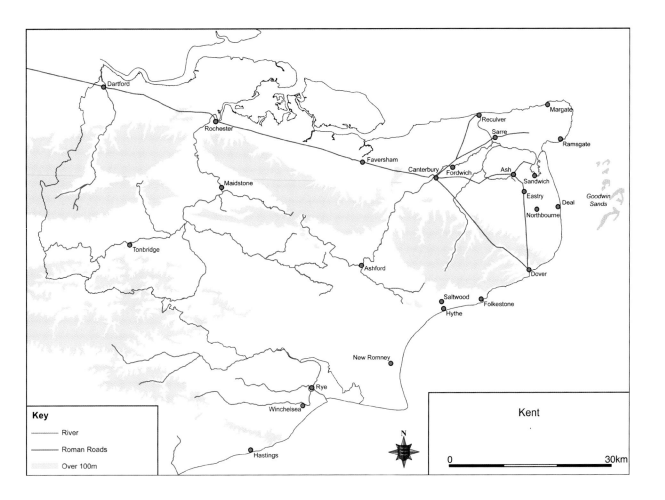

Key

—— River

—— Roman Roads

▨ Over 100m

Kent

0   30km

Figure 1.10 Sandwich and other towns mentioned in the text including all seven Cinque Ports (JH)

(Reproduced by permission of Ordnance Survey on behalf of HMSO. © Crown copyright 2011. All rights reserved. Ordnance Survey Licence number 100046522)

In return for ship service the Cinque Ports enjoyed special privileges including freedom from national taxation, the right of the portsmen to be tried in the ports' own courts of law, and official control of the Great Yarmouth herring fair, one of the most important trading fairs of medieval Europe. Those privileges have all long since been abandoned, but there is still one that is proudly guarded to this day. At each coronation since 1189 the canopy above the monarch has been carried by freemen (also called barons) of the Cinque Ports.

A period of growth and consolidation: the 12th century

In the 11th century written sources and the parish churches are the only things available for understanding what Sandwich was like. By the 12th century they can be fleshed out a little by archaeology, although there has been little opportunity to excavate in this town which is protected as a conservation area.

The town government which began to take shape in the 11th century must have been well established by the 12th century, for as early as 1127 there were townsmen with sufficient experience to serve on a jury that adjudicated in a dispute about land ownership between Christ Church Priory and St Augustine's Abbey, Canterbury. They would have been men who rose to be leaders of the urban administration which was, perhaps unofficially, recognized during the reign of Henry I (1100–35). In the 1150s they felt confident enough to ask Henry II to confirm the rights that his grandfather had bestowed on the town, and this he did.

We do not know how many people lived in the town at this time, but by the end of the century the number must have been considerably greater than the 2,000 of Domesday Book. It was probably well on the way to its medieval peak of something near 5,000, which was reached by around the year 1300. Most residents continued to live in the same type of simple dwelling as their predecessors, and the scanty remains of a house were found when excavating near St Peter's church. It was rectangular, built of wood, with a smoothed clay floor. The house was so flimsily built that it lasted no more than about 50 years before needing to be replaced. This was typical of most of the houses at the time, so demolition and rebuilding along the town streets must have been a common sight. There must have been some grander houses than these, where the town officials and richer tradesmen lived, but the earliest domestic buildings to have survived in Sandwich were built no earlier than the turn of the 13th and 14th centuries.

Demolition and rebuilding were not confined to the houses. In the Christ Church Priory complex at the west end of town an earlier 'great house', perhaps built of timber, was rebuilt in stone. This was a long, two-storey, rectangular building overlooking the Priory's private quay. Its lower storey was a cellar which was probably used as a warehouse for the wine and other luxuries unloaded at the quayside, and above it were a chapel, a great hall and chamber (the living accommodation) and offices of the treasurer and other administrators of the Priory's wealth and lands. The kitchen was probably free-standing, for fear of fire. After the Dissolution of the Monasteries some of the buildings may have been used for Manwood School which was built on the site in 1564 (see Figure 4.7), but all that remains now are some stones from a 13th-century doorway, in a wall at the corner of Paradise Row and Strand Street (Figure 1.11)

The Priory may have left another legacy of great importance: the Delf stream, which is still a feature of the town as it flows alongside New Street and Delf Street. There is no definite proof of who was responsible for it, but its construction was a considerable feat of engineering which the early town is unlikely to have been able to achieve. In contrast, Christ Church Priory had the wealth to fund such an enterprise and also the expertise as it had recently put in a highly elaborate water system in the mother house at Canterbury.

Figure 1.11 Remains of a 13th-century doorway in Paradise Row, probably from the priory's buildings
(HC)

Figure 1.12 (left) The Delf in the town today (HC)

Figure. 1.13 (below) One of the surviving water pumps that served the town in the 19th century. It stands beside the chapel of St Bartholomew's hospital (HC)

We know that the Delf is a man-made watercourse as its name is an Old English word meaning 'ditch', or 'something dug'. Its function was to provide a supply of clean water to the priory, but it must also have supplied the town. Its source was two springs about 5 km south of the town whose waters were diverted to flow through a deliberately dug channel (the Pinnock) leading to the outskirts of Sandwich, and then to the river Stour. As it was (and still is) an open conduit throughout most of its length, it can easily be polluted (Figure 1.12). This was recognized as a problem as early as 1300, but however much the town councils through the ages threatened punishment, for more than eight centuries the townspeople not only drank the water but bathed in it, used it in industries such as tanning, and allowed their domestic animals to wallow in it. By the 19th century the authorities recognized that the water of the Delf must have contributed to the many epidemics which had swept through the town over the years, and so a waterworks was built in 1894 (Figure 1.13).

The three parish churches are the only buildings that remain from 12th-century Sandwich, and they give the impression that it was already a prosperous and well-populated place. They were enlarged and embellished during the second half of the 12th century, the most lavish modifications being at St Clement's and St Mary's which became larger and grander than most churches in Kent at the time.

Figure 1.14 St Clement's 12th-century tower from the south
(GC)

The most visible change was to St Clement's, where the tower was rebuilt in a highly decorated style (Figures 1.14, 1.15). It is so similar to the 12th-century towers of Canterbury cathedral that it may have been built by the same masons. It must have been a spectacular addition to the skyline, and an invaluable landmark to ships sailing into harbour. Some

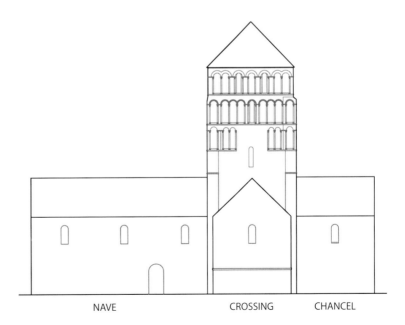

NAVE   CROSSING   CHANCEL

Figure 1.15 Reconstruction of St Clement's church in the 12th century
(HJ/ATA)

Figure 1.16 A tympanum (door head) in St Clement's with carved arcading, interlace, and an animal, probably a stag, at the top right
(GC)

Figure 1.17 Inside St Mary's church today
(JT)

stone carvings inside the church show how grand it was (Figure 1.16). There is less to see at St Mary's which was almost totally destroyed when its medieval tower collapsed in 1668, leaving only the walls standing. There is now just an open space with a single row of wooden columns where stone piers once stood (Fig 1.17). Surprisingly, some small details at the west end of the 12th-century church have survived and they indicate that in the middle of the 12th century there were aisles and a central tower. Parts of two of the stone piers are preserved beneath the present floor, concealed by movable wooden covers. The plan of St Peter's church in the 12th century remains elusive, but it is clear that its nave was extended to its present length sometime in the 1100s.

Timeline 2

Sandwich		General	Reigns	
Rights confirmed by King John	1205		1199–1217	John
	1215–17	1st Barons' War		
St Bartholomew's hospital founded	1217	Battle of Sandwich		
Town supports Simon de Montfort	1259–67	2nd Barons' War	1216–72	Henry III
	1260	Cinque Ports formalized		
Castle first mentioned as royal	1266			
Carmelite friary founded	1268			
	1276	Cinque Ports a single unit in law	1272–1307	Edward I
St John's hospital founded	1280s			
Crown takes over from Christ Church Priory	1290	Liberties of Cinque Ports established		
	1298	Liberties confirmed		
Population peaks at c.5,000	c.1300			
Custumal	1300/1301			

Developments in Sandwich *c.*1200–*c.*1300 set against major events in the history of England

2 Towards a well organized town: Sandwich by *c*.1300

In the 13th century the written sources begin to tell us more about the people of the town and their activities. We know the names of some of the tradesmen and artisans who worked at everyday jobs in the town, but the wealthy merchants have left us even more information. They grew rich on the proceeds of the wholesale import and export trade on which the prosperity of Sandwich depended and which was then at its height. For the first time we can get some idea of how they lived, for parts of some of their grand houses can still be seen. They spent their riches on building them in stone, but some merchants also donated towards worthy causes such as hospitals for the poor and needy and a Carmelite friary.

The Custumal

Much the clearest picture of 13th-century Sandwich is given by its Custumal, written in *c*.1300. By then Sandwich had become a fairly large town in medieval terms, with a population of about 5,000, a town council of jurats (town councillors) and an elected mayor. Its administration also included a lawyer and a town clerk (who was also a lawyer). Together they compiled a legal document called a Custumal, in which the customs and usages of the town were written down. They had previously been transmitted by word of mouth, but once written down officially they became legal documents which were much easier to consult and defend. As might be expected, much of the Custumal is devoted to legal matters and urban governance, but it also gives details of everyday life which show what sort of place Sandwich had developed into by the end of the 13th century.

By the time of the Custumal Sandwich had had some form of local government for over a century, with a mayor chosen every year by the jurats. It was now laid down that the mayor was to be elected annually at a meeting in St Clement's church, and other council officers at another meeting, in

St Peter's. The town council was highly organized, with many of the officials holding positions that still have their modern equivalents, such as the treasurer (finance), the serjeant (law and order), the warden for orphans (social services) and the common weigher (trading standards).

The treasurer's job became increasingly onerous throughout the Middle Ages, mainly because the town acquired more and more property. Some, such as the hospitals mentioned above (and see page 35), were a drain on the civic purse, others such as houses, shops, watermills and the town crane, were leased out for commercial gain. The treasurer kept the books, and because he was accountable if the moneys did not add up, the post was often difficult to fill. Similarly, it was sometimes difficult to persuade a jurat to stand for election as mayor, for the mayor himself had to fund the various banquets and junketings that were an integral part of the office. At one stage, a jurat who refused to be nominated was threatened with the demolition of his house. A rather extreme measure, one might think.

The town serjeant, on the other hand, had no such expenses, but lots of responsibility. His job involved checking who came into the town on market days and what they were bringing with them. Most traders would have been transporting agricultural produce from the farms in the neighbourhood to the markets which were held in the High Street near St Clement's church and Fishmarket near St Peter's. Both market places are still there. Fishmarket is now known as Market Street but is in the same position as always, although the riverbank was once much closer to it. The market place in the High Street ceased to function before the end of the Middle Ages and all that remains to remind us of it are its curving sides, giving it a slight cigar-shape which is characteristic of medieval market places (Figure 2.1).

The serjeant was also in charge of the fifteen men who made up the night watch. Some of them patrolled the streets during the hours of darkness, and others were stationed at strategic points along the river bank. They kept an eye on the traffic on the river and ships anchored in the Haven, but were mainly concerned with catching petty criminals who were then sent before the mayor, who was also the town magistrate, sitting in his weekly court in St Peter's church. Those found guilty might be thrown into the town gaol near St Peter's church, or perhaps sentenced for a spell in the stocks that probably stood on Strand Street near Pillory Gate. He also had to ensure that proper fire precautions were taken. In dry weather there had to be a tub of

Figure 2.1 High Street from the air. The slight widening shows where temporary stalls could be erected for markets and fairs

(EH NRM 24073/15)

water by the entrance to each house and the lanes leading to the river at Pillory Gate, St Mary Gate and Ives Gate which opened onto the riverside had always to be empty enough for access to the water to be unobstructed.

The Custumal indicates that the mayor and jurats were jointly responsible for law and order, and for the wellbeing of the townspeople, including the upkeep of the urban infrastructure. For instance, it was decreed that the streets should 'be kept clear of dung, timber and other nuisances that may obstruct passengers either on foot or on horseback'. There were many and varied 'nuisances'. One complaint was that pigs 'ran about the streets without a person to take care of them'. This was strictly forbidden, presumably to no avail as the same complaint is lodged throughout the Middle Ages. Butchers were also frequent offenders. They had to be told not to slaughter and gut their animals in the street, but to do it in a quiet and private place where they could not be seen. This place may have been near the river, for they had to dispose of the offal in the river at low tide, at night, and 'in such a cautious manner as may give no public offence'. This injunction was as ineffective as the one against pigs, for the butchers continued to dump rubbish in the river whenever they wished, throwing it into the water from Pillory Gate. By 1558 things had got so bad that Pillory Gate needed refurbishment, 'due to having been a dumping place by the butchers' guild'. Nothing changed, though, for in 1572 there was a decree that the butchers should not dump offal at Pillory Gate until after Elizabeth I's visit to the town, and in 1591 the butchers' guild was again asked to cleanse and repair it. There is no reason to suppose that the state of affairs improved for the next couple of centuries when the problem was solved by Pillory Gate being demolished in 1776.

There was also the perennial problem of the Delf, which was the sole responsibility of the mayor and jurats 'from the spring head or well to its mouth'. They must have despaired of keeping the water pure, but despite increasingly desperate injunctions, washerwomen kept rinsing their washing and scouring out their washtubs in it, and many worse things were deposited in it. The Council also expected the serjeant to keep fowl away from the Delf, but it is difficult to see how he could be responsible for that, and ducks still love the Delf today (Figure 2.2). The pollution was obviously appalling.

The Custumal tells us more about the most unpleasant aspects of the town – filthy streets, polluted water – than we might like, but it also shows the mayor and jurats in a very positive light. This Council was not just interested in collecting taxes; it genuinely wanted the town to be a decent place to live in. One thing that the mayor and jurats promised would have made that snapshot even more detailed and uniquely helpful. The Custumal states,

> The mayor and jurats should, at least once in every seven years as has been the custom, take a careful survey of all parts of the town, and observe whether there are any encroachments or obstructions at the passages leading to the river, or in the streets, [such] as in building upon the footpath, in covering any watercourse, in holding and occupying any spot of ground belonging to the public, in having a drain of filth from any house to the Delf, or over the street.

This suggests that the town had already been surveyed every seven years for a considerable length of time, 'as has been the custom', and promises to continue to do so. Unfortunately, no surveys survive in the Sandwich records; have they been lost, or was the promise not kept? We shall probably never know. Instead we have to rely on the evidence that has been preserved, such as the architecture of the churches and the hospital, the few domestic buildings that have left us their remains, and the gradually growing number of surviving written records.

Figure 2.2 A duck on the Delf in 2011

(HC)

The urban environment

The 13th century saw many changes in the appearance of the town. Churches were no longer the only stone buildings; there were new masonry buildings in the friary, St Bartholomew's hospital and the well-established Priory buildings at the west side of town. By the end of the century the religious buildings no longer had a monopoly on stone and some rich merchants began to put up stone houses in the streets close to the river. Stone must have been an exorbitantly expensive building material as it all had to be brought to Sandwich from a distance. Ragstone from quarries near Maidstone and Folkestone, flint from the North and South Downs, and disused masonry from the abandoned Roman settlements of Richborough and Reculver were all employed in Sandwich buildings, but the most prized and highest status stone was fine limestone from Caen in Normandy. All were brought in at considerable expense, but even so were less costly than brick, which was a rarity as it was not made in England until the 15th century. In the 13th century it came into Sandwich from The Netherlands where there already were brickworks, and may have been brought over the North Sea as ballast in merchant ships.

The excavations near St Peter's church showed that by the end of the 13th century even rather simple houses were built with stone walls, and fragments of masonry built into walls around the town suggest that this was fairly common. In addition, there are more substantial remains of two stone buildings, one of them a ruin and the other much changed but still lived in. They were both built about the year 1300. The ruinous one is the small structure in Three Kings Yard, on the south side of Strand Street. It originally stood at one side of a courtyard, which probably had timber buildings on the other three sides. The stone building is rectangular and of two storeys, a storage room for valuable goods below and the owner's private apartment above. Its walls are rubble built (Figure 2.3), except for

Figure 2.3 (below left)
A stone building in Three Kings Yard (part of The Chanter's House, Strand Street) dating from about 1300
(HC)

Figure 2.4 (below right)
Caen stone and Low Countries bricks used in a window in Three Kings Yard
(JT)

Figure 2.5A 20 High Street
(the white house on the
right of the picture) and
Pellicane House

(GC)

Figure 2.5B   Cross section
of 20 High Street showing
that it was a hall open to
the roof

(ATA)

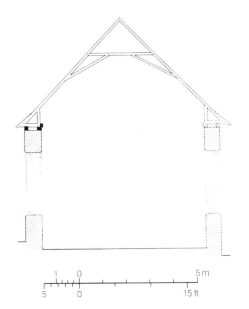

1   0   5 m

5   0   15 ft

the corners and facings of the windows, which are of
Caen stone. Bricks imported from The Netherlands
were also used (Figure 2.4). It would have been a neat
little building when it was completed, with the rubble
and brick plastered and whitewashed but the Caen
stone details left exposed to show that the owner was
someone who could afford such things. In contrast, 20
High Street looks like a stuccoed late-medieval timber-
framed house, but its interior shows that it is part
of a great stone-walled open hall, most of which was
demolished when its neighbour, Pellicane House, was
rebuilt in the early 17th century (Figure 2.5A). What
remains, though, is very unusual in that it has survived
to its full height, showing us how spacious late 13th-
century houses could have been (Figure 2.5B).

What was perhaps the most magnificent stone house in the town is represented by only a stretch of its front wall, now a garden wall in Harnet Street. Part of the Caen stone moulding around a blocked doorway and an expanse of exquisitely executed knapped flint are all that remains of the main entrance to a large merchant's house (Figures 2.6 & 2.7A). The flint work is a technique that was most often used in churches (Figure 2.7B) and in a secular building is a sign of conspicuous wealth. Unfortunately we don't know the name of the great merchant who lived there when it was built around 1300, but by the middle of the 14th century it belonged to a family called Gibbon, who by then were long established and prosperous merchants. So the Gibbons could have owned it from the start.

Figure 2.6 Exquisitely knapped flint in a garden wall in Harnet Street

(GC)

Figure 2.7A Detail showing the high standard of flint knapping in Harnet Street

(GC)

Figure 2.7B (far right) Detail of the less well executed knapped flint in the west wall of St Mary's church

(GC)

The people who lived in these houses were the elite of Sandwich. They were all prosperous and part of the urban establishment, with the men serving as jurats and then as mayors. They lived close together in certain areas of the town such as Strand Street and near St Mary's church. They were often related by marriage and everyone knew everyone else. Some had risen from humble roots, which they did not forget, for many of them were generous to the poor. But all of them had grown wealthy through trade.

Sources of wealth

The main import was wine, brought over from Bordeaux, the centre of a wine-growing district on the banks of the river Gironde in south-west France. This region, plus a huge area stretching from Bayonne in the south almost to the river Loire in the north, and right across to the Auvergne in the east, had been in English hands since 1152 when Eleanor of Aquitaine married the future Henry II. From then on, for about 200 years, the English kings were also dukes of Gascony and Aquitaine. They frequently sailed to France from Sandwich and other southern ports, which benefited from having the royal retinue passing through. Many of the ports also profited from handling the great volume of wine which was imported for royal, aristocratic and ecclesiastical households, and increasingly for the wealthier members of society.

Sandwich's part in this trade was mainly as a place where the wine was transferred from the cargo carriers to smaller ships. It was then taken to London through the Wantsum Channel and along the Thames estuary, or conveyed along the river Stour to the religious houses in Canterbury. Some wine stayed in Sandwich, either to be sent to the Lord Warden at Dover Castle, or to be drunk by the rich merchants who appreciated the finer things of life. The wine was also accompanied by other delicacies such as almonds and figs, which would grace only the very richest tables. In contrast, there is one record of whale meat, or perhaps blubber, being brought in on a Portuguese ship and then distributed to some Spanish and Portuguese merchants who were living and working in Sandwich at the time.

Less exotic goods were sent out in exchange. The main English export in the 13th century was wool, which was famed for its high quality and greatly in demand on the Continent. Bales of raw wool were shipped to Sandwich, either from local sources which produced the Kentish speciality of lambswool or from Yorkshire and Lincolnshire, and then loaded onto cargo vessels to be taken overseas. Bundles of cattle hides from local herds were supplemented by others from further afield, and grain was also brought to the town, mainly from the fertile arable fields of east Kent.

Sandwich Haven and its ships

All this activity meant that Sandwich's quaysides and the anchorage of the Haven were busy with cargo vessels from many English and Continental ports. Three different types of ships would have dominated. Two of these would have been cumbersome sailing ships built in north-west Europe as cargo carriers: the hulk and the cog, known colloquially as 'roundships' (Figures 2.8 and 2.9). The third type would have been the galley, which originated in France and the Mediterranean. Galleys were basically rowing boats, although they could hoist a sail when necessary. They were shallow-draught 'longships', much speedier than the hulks and cogs but not very useful as freighters. Their main role was as warships, and English kings maintained a few of them to make up the royal fleets in the 13th and 14th centuries. When the port of Bayonne on the French Atlantic coast was in English hands all the galleys used by the English kings were made there. There were never very many of them as they were enormously expensive to build and also to maintain. When out of service they were kept and looked after in boathouses in Rye and Winchelsea. But there was no permanent berth or boathouse for them in Sandwich even though in times of war it

Figure 2.8 Hulk shown on the 14th-century seal of Sandwich
(RH, SGA)

Figure 2.9 Reconstruction drawing of a cog (Clarke et al. 2010, fig. 5.7)

was common for galleys to be summoned to the Haven where the king and his forces would embark.

Very often the merchantmen that gathered in Sandwich Haven may have been preparing for war rather than trade. The country did not have a navy such as we have today, the only national fleet being the few royal galleys. What were really needed in the foreign wars of the Middle Ages were sturdy vessels which could transport armies and their equipment. Campaigns were generally fought on land, not on the high seas, so fighting ships were seldom employed. When a fleet of troop transports was needed, the usual way was to press merchant vessels into service; this was an ancient right exercised by the sovereign and apparently not questioned by his subjects even though it played havoc with their commercial activities. Once in the place of assembly, they were modified to carry men and horses rather than wool, grain or timber. This is what happened in 1297 when the Lord Warden of the Cinque Ports summoned ships to Sandwich to prepare for war against Scotland. Once there, the ships drew up near the castle (see below) where they were fitted out. Special bridges replaced gangplanks so that horses could be taken on board, and loose boxes were contrived out of wickerwork hurdles to keep the animals safe during the voyage. Ships had also been summoned to meet in the mouth of the river Orwell near Harwich, Essex, and to sail from there to join the Sandwich contingent. There were 305 ships in all, and the fleet must have been a very grand sight as it set out.

The Crown and the castle

Since 1023 the monks of Christ Church Priory had profited greatly from the rights granted to them by Canute, but in 1290 they exchanged these with the king for ready cash and property in the Kent countryside. So the Crown took over the Priory's role and appointed a bailiff to look after the royal interests in the town. His most important duties were to maintain the law of the land by presiding over his own court, held every week in St Clement's church, and to collect the customs dues charged on the foreign ships that called at the port and unloaded their cargoes there.

The Crown often paid lip service to the town by appointing a local resident as bailiff, invariably someone from one of the wealthy families who dominated local government. Their administrative headquarters was the castle, which we first hear about in 1266 when it was besieged by supporters of Henry III during the Second Barons' War (a civil war between the king and rebellious lords led by Simon de Montfort). That is the first time that the castle is mentioned in written records and the only time that it came under attack. It never became one of the great royal castles with defensive

Figure 2.10 Castle Field seen from Mill Wall
(GC)

capabilities, that role was left to Dover, but until the town took it over at the end of the 15th century it remained an administrative centre used by the royal bailiff in his day-to-day business, and also by monarchs who passed through Sandwich on their way overseas. The name 'Castle Field' is all that remains to remind us where it once stood, east of St Clement's church and on land that belonged to the Crown from Anglo-Saxon times until the Civil War in the 17th century (Figure 2.10).

Archaeology is our only source for knowing what the castle looked like in its first hundred years. Then it was a simple earth and timber structure surrounded by a ditch. In was not until the late 14th century that it acquired a few stone buildings (page 48). When it was built there were no walls or ramparts around Sandwich, and the castle and town would have been one unit. It was not until the great earth rampart of Mill Wall was built in the 1330s that the castle was cut off from the town. We shall see below how the separation of castle and town proved a blessing in disguise during the Hundred Years' War.

The religious houses and churches

Hospitals, really almshouses rather than hospitals in the sense that we know them today, were a common feature of many medieval towns. They provided homes for the aged and less well off, but not for the absolutely destitute, and two were built in Sandwich in the 13th century. The first to be built was St Bartholomew's hospital, founded in 1217 in thanksgiving for the king's victory in the Battle of Sandwich, a sea battle that ended the First Barons' War (between King John and his barons). The battle took place on St Bartholomew's day (24th August), hence the dedication to that saint. The hospital may originally have been designed to care for mariners wounded in the battle, but it soon became home to twelve men and four women who each paid an entrance fee of £10. Each resident had a room of his or her own, in return for working in the house or garden. Although the aristocratic Sir Henry de Sandwich and the merchants Bertine de Crawthorne and William Burcharde paid for its foundation, by the end of the century the town council was responsible for running it, as it still does today. It is now an almshouse, with individual and much modified cottages for residents (Figure 2.11), but it still has its splendid 13th-century chapel (Figure 2.12).

St Bartholomew's stands a little apart from the town proper. It is 1km south of the river, beside the road into town from Eastry and Dover. Its siting seems to have been carefully planned, for it is also on the slightly higher Thanet Beds beyond the alluvial ground south of the Delf. As mentioned above, the Alluvium needed to be drained before it could be settled, and it may be significant that when St Bartholomew's was built in the early 13th century it avoided land that must still have been too wet for occupation. That ground must have been drained towards the end of the 13th century, when St John's hospital was founded on the Alluvium just south of the Delf. The benefactors of St John's hospital included the wool merchant Thomas Shelving from one of the richest and most influential families in the town, John de Ho (mayor in 1296 and 1299) who lived in the prestigious area by the Priory's site, much favoured by the wealthy, and John Long, a ship owner. Although they founded it, the cost of its upkeep, as with St Bartholomew's, soon fell on the town council who continued to house twelve townspeople there.

Once the land south of the Delf was drained Sandwich's only friary, a house of Carmelites or Whitefriars, was set up there (see Figure 1.7A). In 1268 Henry Coufeld donated land to the Carmelites, on which they built their friary to house no more than 24 friars. The end part of Henry's name was 'de Alemania' (of Germany), which suggests that he was a foreign merchant resident in Sandwich, but we know nothing more about him than his name. As mentioned in Chapter 1, it was not unusual for landowners to give the poorer parts of their properties to charity, and this gift of ground that was perhaps only partially dried-out is typical. The site was also typical of friaries in that it lay just outside the town boundary, which at that time was the Delf as The Rope Walk rampart had not been built by then.

Nothing of the friary buildings remains above ground as they were demolished at the Dissolution of the Monasteries, but archaeological excavations in the area of the Guildhall Car Park have revealed the plan of the friars' medieval church and living quarters, all built of stone (Figure 2.13). They stood within a precinct that was surrounded by a moat, mainly to keep out the outside world but also, and probably not just accidentally, to help the friary site to dry out more quickly. When the friary was first founded it probably relied on the Delf for its water, but it soon acquired its own supply, which must have been much purer that that on

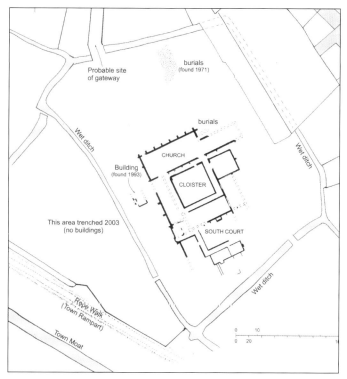

which the townspeople depended. In 1306 the rich wool merchant Thomas Shelving, who had helped found St John's hospital a couple of decades earlier, bequeathed to the friary a plot of land in Woodnesborough, a village about 2km away, where there was a spring. An underground conduit was then constructed to carry water from the spring to the friary. The friars must have been the envy of the town, and much healthier than most of the Sandwich people.

By the time that the friary and St John's hospital were founded, the area between them may already have been used as a market place. The highway from Woodnesborough (Moat Sole) ran through it to a bridge over the Delf and the centre of town, making it an ideal place for buying and selling locally grown grain (hence its medieval name of Cornmarket) and locally bred sheep and cattle. Its present name of Cattle Market reflects its use into the 20th century (Figure 2.14).

Figure 2.14 The Cattle Market (medieval Cornmarket) painted in 1906 by H. Morris Page and now hanging in the Guildhall

(SGA)

At the end of the 13th century Sandwich was a fine, prosperous town with many stone dwelling houses and religious buildings. Its castle was small

but probably adequate for the demands made upon it by the bailiff and occasional royal visitors. The Haven was the destination of great ships carrying wine and other precious goods, and the townsfolk benefited from these overseas contacts and conducted business in three market places. The following century proved to be more problematic for Sandwich and its inhabitants.

Timeline 3

Sandwich		General	Reigns	
The name of a female baker (Matilda de Davyes gate) is the first evidence any gate in Sandwich	1300		1307–27	Edward II
Custumal	1300/1301			
Davis Quay first mentioned	1300/1301			
Genoese, Venetian & other great merchant ships frequent Haven	Early 1300s			
First murage grant	1321			
MPs chosen from town elite	1327	Parliament starts to meet almost every year	1327–77	Edward III
Ramparts built	1330s			
Tree-ring date for 39 Strand Street	1334			
Sandwich Haven an assembly point for fleets	1337–1453	Hundred Years' War Periods of war & peace		
	1340	English victory at Sluys		
	1347	English victory at Crécy		
Becomes port for provisioning Calais	1347	English capture Calais		
Population probably halved	1348–50	Black Death		
	1360	Treaty of Bretigny interrupts hostilities		
	1361–2, 1369, 1375	Black Death recurrences		
	1370s	Hundred Years' War hostilities begin again		
Much building at castle	1380s		1377–99	Richard II
Fisher Gate built in stone	1380s			
Stone walls on river bank begun	1380s	Periods of war & peace		
St Thomas's hospital founded	1392			
	1407		1399–1415	Henry IV
	1415	Civil war in France English victory at Agincourt	1415–22	Henry V
			1422–61	Henry VI
			(1422–37 Regency Council)	
	1431	Henry VI crowned king of France		
Haven begins to silt up, no longer visited by foreign merchant vessels	mid 1400s			
Suffers economically from end of hostilities	1453	End of war, Calais only English possession		

Developments in Sandwich c.1300–c.1450 set against major events in the history of England

3   Sandwich survives disease, death and war: from *c*.1300 to the early 1400s

With a few exceptions, this whole period was a time of great trouble for England, and for the Continent as a whole. In the early years of the century unseasonal weather caused crops to fail and a fatal animal disease called the murrain attacked herds of cattle and flocks of sheep. This led to the Great Famine of 1315–17, which so undermined the health of the population that when the Black Death struck 30 years later many people were in no state to combat it. The Hundred Years' War with France, which began before the Black Death and continued sporadically for more than its hundred years, also blighted England's economy. But, in contrast, the 14th century was not such a depressed time for Sandwich. This was largely because the Haven was an important assembly point for warships setting off for France, and also, once Calais became an English enclave, Sandwich played a pivotal role in keeping it manned and provisioned.

Sandwich before the Hundred Years' War

Most inhabitants of Sandwich were people of modest means, about whom we know little except that they pursued the trades and crafts vital to the functioning of a medieval town, occasionally paid taxes, and were sometimes summoned to a court of law for usually minor offences. Their surnames may reflect their occupations: brewer, butcher, butler, carpenter, chandler, cook, cooper, cutler, draper, glover, goldsmith, skinner, smith, tiler and many more that we would still recognize today. The names may also tell us where the people lived, or where they or their ancestors came from. For example, Matilda and William de Davyesgate probably lived near the gate onto the quay roughly where The Barbican now stands; and Stephan de Hardres may well have come from the village of that name south of Canterbury.

No houses of the poor have survived and even those of the more prosperous are rarely preserved, but Sandwich is very fortunate in having three merchants' houses from the early 14th century. This was a time when stone became less fashionable, or too expensive, for domestic buildings so timber framing was used instead. The three Sandwich examples were probably the residences of rich merchants who were benefiting from the minor economic upturn that Sandwich experienced in the early decades of the century (see below).

The houses, Numbers 33, 39 and 41 Strand Street, stand on the side further from the river (Figure 3.1A). They were built in the 1330s in a location ideal for merchants who specialized in importing and exporting goods by ship. There were no dwellings houses between them and the river, so each merchant's house would have opened onto its own quay, with a hoist for loading and offloading and perhaps a warehouse. At the time, the land where Strand Street now runs had only recently been reclaimed from the river so the street itself was probably more like a track or lane than a formal urban street.

The houses themselves contained as many as nine rooms but we don't know if any of them were used for domestic purposes only. They were primarily store rooms and shops, but could also have been used to sleep in. The family's main living space was a single tall room, known as a hall, with no ceiling to obscure the timber rafters that supported the tiled roof (Figure 3.1B). It was sparsely furnished, basically with a table and a couple of benches, and perhaps cupboards. Heat, and most of the light, came from a hearth in the middle of the floor, the smoke from it permeating everything in the vicinity. This was the only heated room, and was where both the household and visitors would have gathered. The hearth may have been used for cooking too, but the grander houses may have had a separate kitchen.

If you think that the home life of the medieval merchant was not cosy, just imagine how much worse it must have been for the lower orders!

Sandwich enjoyed something of a boom early in the 14th century. Until trade was disrupted by the outbreak of the Hundred Years War in 1337, the merchants who built these impressive houses were the import-export traders of their day, specialising in importing luxury foodstuffs from abroad. Honey, figs, grapes, raisins, dates and almonds were brought in by Spanish

Figure 3.1A Numbers 39 and 41 Strand Street, the earliest timber-framed houses in Sandwich dated to 1334 by tree-ring dating
(JT)

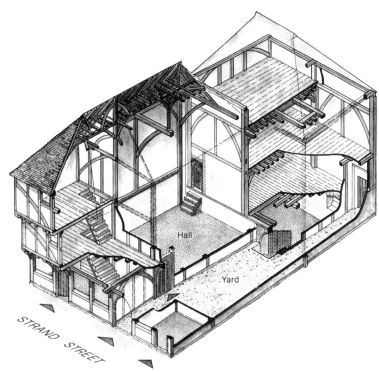

Figure 3.1B Reconstruction of the interior of 39 Strand Street when it was built
(ATA)

merchants, and wine came from Gascony. More essential, but still very valuable, goods were also imported: silver, copper and tin from Majorca, rabbit and badger skins, leather and hides from northern Spain, woad from France and Italy, salt from the Bay of Bourgneuf (an inlet off the Bay of Biscay), and soft wood from the pine forests around the Baltic Sea. These things, too, were mainly shipped on from Sandwich, although some would have been kept in the town. Salt was especially desirable, and that from Bourgneuf was rated the best of all.

On their return journey, the cargo ships would have carried basic agricultural products such as wool, grain, cheese and butter, mostly from the immediate surroundings or slightly further afield in Kent and Sussex. Wool was shipped to Sandwich from the West Country and Yorkshire, and coal was brought down from Newcastle.

Sandwich and the Hundred Years' War (1337–1453)

A summary of the progress of the war

At the beginning of the war the French dominated the English Channel, disrupting trade by attacking cargo vessels and carrying out or threatening raids on the south and south-east coasts, including Sandwich and other Cinque Ports. But this dominance was broken in 1340 when Edward III defeated the French at the sea battle of Sluys, off the Flemish coast near Bruges. He then went on to victory at Crécy in 1346, and in 1347 the port of Calais fell to the English after a year-long siege. By 1360 the Treaty of Bretigny brought peace and confirmed England's hold over most of south-west France.

Less than ten years later the war started again. Royal fleets carrying armed troops sailed out of Sandwich, and in the 1360s and 1370s French privateers raided ports along the Channel coast. The French progressively won back much of the land that they had lost by the 1360 treaty, but in 1407 a civil war in France gave England the opportunity to win it back again. Thanks largely to Shakespeare, this campaign is best known through Henry V's victory at Agincourt in 1415. By 1420 most of northern France was in English hands, and it was agreed that Henry V should be crowned in Paris as king of France, thus becoming sovereign of the two countries simultaneously. But he died before his French coronation, and in 1422 was succeeded by his infant son

Henry VI, who was barely nine months old. A regency council governed for him until 1437, although he was crowned king of England in 1429 and of France in 1431. Even when he reached adulthood he proved incapable of ruling either country, and certainly not of holding on to what his father had gained. During his turbulent reign weak government at home and poor leadership in France led to the loss of Gascony in 1453, by which time the only English possession in France was Calais. It remained in English hands until 1558.

Sandwich Haven

When the Hundred Years' War began, overseas trade was disrupted by enemy action and piracy, and also by the demands made by the Crown on merchant shipping. More and more merchantmen were called into the king's service to act as troopships in the military campaigns against France, so their peaceful trading was frequently disrupted. Nevertheless, Sandwich seems to have weathered the economic storms of the 14th century better than many other English towns.

After 1347 Calais became the chief port of entry and exit for the armies deployed in France, and Sandwich began to benefit from the war. Calais was only about 60km away across the English Channel, and although Dover to Calais was a shorter crossing, Dover's harbour was man-made, small and exposed, more suited to single vessels than to flotillas. In contrast, Sandwich's Haven provided calm water and space enough for a fleet of ships to assemble in safety while being loaded with the troops, horses, provisions and general baggage needed to wage a war. So it naturally became the main port of embarkation.

Most of the ships that set out from Sandwich Haven were merchantmen, modified to take troops, equipment and livestock. Occasionally the ships are described as cogs or hulks, but more often only their size is given. In the early decades of the 14th century, ships of all sizes between 50 and 180 tuns were commandeered, the *tun* being the unit of measurement used. We still talk about 'tonnage' of ships today, and this term derives from the medieval wine trade. Wine imported from Gascony came in by the 'tun', that is, a barrel big enough to contain at least 252 gallons (about 1,000 litres).

Figure 3.2 Cogs used as warships. Shown in an early 14th-century manuscript

(© The British Library Board. Royal 10 E IV f.19)

This was a standard measurement of volume, and by the beginning of the 14th century it became the convention to estimate the size of a ship by the number of tuns that it could carry as cargo – usually recorded as 'xxx tuns burden'. So, when the king wanted to summon ships of a certain size for war, he would specify the tunnage of the ships that he needed. During the Hundred Years' War most of the ships that had been commandeered for military service and gathered in Sandwich Haven were between 50 and 120 tuns, summoned there 'from Bristol to the mouth of the Thames' or 'from Newcastle to Sandwich'. The summonses became increasingly desperate during the 15th century when the war was taking a turn for the worse, until in 1453 'all ships above the portage [burden] of 20 tuns' were called to go to Bordeaux, to evacuate the troops. This is reminiscent of the fleet of 'little ships' of Dunkirk in 1940.

After Calais fell to the English, Sandwich Haven was busy with supply ships waiting for favourable winds. There must have been constant movement of men and vessels, and demands for provisions and services which the townspeople could provide. The richer merchants of Sandwich also took advantage of the troop movements, as can be seen from the story of 'insider dealing' in surplus provisions originally intended for the fleet headed for Sluys (see page 57).

Sandwich was also a base for some of the vessels belonging to the Crown. There were not very many of them, but they were repaired and maintained there while riding at anchor or in docks beside the castle. In 1355 carpenters and shipwrights were summoned to build a dock in which to repair the royal ship *George*, and in 1357 Sandwich was the headquarters of the royal fleet, with fourteen of the king's ships based there. The next two years were particularly busy, for Edward III was planning to invade France once again. Hundreds of troops marched eastwards through Kent, disrupting other road users and overwhelming the inns along the highways. Innkeepers were warned that they should sell food and drink to the soldiers at a reasonable price, but it is difficult to believe that they didn't take advantage of such an opportunity for exploitation. They certainly did in Rochester, where sour wine was deliberately sold to the troops. The congestion on the highways must have been unimaginable. In one year archers were marching along them in July, soldiers were heading for Sandwich in August, and when they arrived they all had to camp out in the castle grounds until the fleet was ready to sail in October. The merchants whose ships had been forced to join the fighting fleet complained that they lost money because their vessels were kept idle for months before sailing, and it is easy to see why. The logistics of getting all the troops to Sandwich on foot along dusty or muddy roads already thronging with carts carrying hurdles, bridges, chests full of bows, arrows, quivers and crossbows, and with herds of cattle and flocks of sheep being driven to Sandwich, would tax the most efficient bureaucrat. Little wonder that nothing happened on time.

Sandwich Castle

Even before the war officially broke out, there was a depot at Sandwich where cattle were kept after having been brought in on the hoof from many parts of England, and there were also warehouses for grain shipped down river from Essex and north Kent. Hurdles and other fittings used to transform merchantmen into horse transports and troop carriers were also brought in. We do not know where the depot was, but it was probably in the grounds of the castle, on the south bank of the Haven where the ships waited to be loaded.

Sandwich Castle came into its own during the war, becoming the embarkation point for kings, such as Edward III, Henry IV and Henry VI, and their armies. As we have seen thousands of troops and their horses bivouacked in the castle grounds, piles of arms and equipment waited to be loaded on board, warehouses were packed with provisions, and herds of cattle and flocks of sheep added to the confusion. The fields around the castle must have been pandemonium for months at a time as the troops waited for their transport ships to be made ready. The townsfolk would have been relieved to have the rampart of Mill Wall as a barrier between them and a rowdy and potentially riotous army.

It is frustrating to know so little about the castle buildings themselves as they played such an important part in the defence of the realm in the 14th and 15th centuries. Most of our information about the castle comes from a few royal documents, one of which tells us that in 1345 there was a chamber fit for King Edward III to stay in before he set out for France. A gaol is the next thing to be mentioned, and then in 1385 a new council chamber was built in stone. The stone walls found by excavation may have been part of this. The next year money was spent on a drawbridge over the moat, a new gate, and a tower. This was a quiet time in the Hundred Years' War, and perhaps the castle was being refurbished while awaiting the next round. The next time repairs are mentioned is in 1440 when Henry VI paid the wages of 'stonecutters, masons, carpenters, plumbers ... and other workmen'.

After the war, the castle reverted to its original administrative role, was taken over by the town, and finally became redundant. It was demolished at the end of Henry VIII's reign, when the nearby castles of Sandown, Deal and Walmer were built. A single tower was spared until the 1890s, when the last vestiges were swept away. Despite its royal status and pivotal role in the defence of England for more than a hundred years, it is forgotten by most Sandwich inhabitants, and even disregarded by medieval military historians.

Town walls

Rather surprisingly for a town that was one of the first in line for attacks from overseas, Sandwich was unprotected by walls until the 14th century. Elsewhere in England, particularly where there were outside threats, from the Welsh for example, walls were being built by the early decades of the 13th century, but Sandwich was not defended until a hundred years later.

The first image labels visible: St Bartholomew's, Site of Castle, Mill Wall, The Rope Walk, The Butts

Figure 3.3 Air view showing the route of the 14th century earth ramparts and the site of the castle and St Bartholomew's hospital which were both cut off from the town when the ramparts were built

(EH NMR 24064/03)

The first documented date for walls at Sandwich is 1321, when a tax was levied to raise money for building them (called a 'murage grant'). This was probably spent on some of the 1km of earth banks, The Rope Walk and the Butts and Mill Wall, which still run round the historic centre of the town (Figure 3.3). The Rope Walk and The Butts were probably in existence as part of a drainage scheme by the time of the murage grant when they may have been strengthened to make them defensible. At the same time they

Figure 3.4A (left)
Looking west along
The Rope Walk
(HC)

Figure 3.4B (right)
Mill Wall looking north
(GC)

were supplemented by Mill Wall, which was newly built for defence alone. It is completely different from The Rope Walk and The Butts (Figure 3.4A) in being a massive earthwork (Figure 3.4B), constructed on the highest part of the Thanet Beds ridge rather than on flat and wet Alluvium. It protected the most vulnerable side of the town, close to the Haven and open to potential attack from the sea. It also drastically changed Sandwich's communications with the south by cutting across the main roads from Worth, Deal and Dover. This turned two lengths of road inside the walls into the cul-de-sacs Millwall Place and Knightrider Street. As a result, the area of the town around St Clement's church became something of a backwater, the High Street market began to decline, and the focus of economic activity moved to the Fishmarket and the Cornmarket, and St Peter's parish in general. This difference in the character of the areas around the churches is still obvious today (Figure 3.5).

Threats from French warships in the 1370s and invasion scares in 1385 and 1386 must have underlined the need to defend the riverside, which had been unguarded until then. In a policy of self-help, the townspeople were called upon to fortify their own property, perhaps with finances from the murage grant issued in 1385. The next year 'masons, carpenters and other artificers, workmen and other labourers' were sent to Sandwich 'for fortifying and walling' with stone and timber, and this was being done at the same time as the castle was undergoing repairs. Some remains of the walls which were built then can be seen along The Quay, but the best preserved survival from

Figure 3.5 St Peter's church (above) stands in a tiny churchyard, surrounded by tightly packed houses whereas St Clement's might almost be a country church

(EH NMR 24073/13 & 14)

Figure 3.6 Fisher Gate on The Quay, built in the 1380s; the brick gable was added in 1581

(JT)

that time is Fisher Gate, a stone gateway which stands at the north end of Quay Lane (Figure 3.6). It was well equipped to guard the entrance into the town from the harbour for its central passage could be closed off by heavy wooden doors and a portcullis which could be lowered at times of attack. Only the lower two storeys date from this time, the upper part of yellow brick with a diamond-shaped decoration was added in about 1500, and the gable above it was built in 1581.

Figure 3.7 (above)
Fragment of the town
wall in the basement
of the Bell Hotel. The
wall was built with two
faces of good stone
and the cavity between
them filled with flint
and mortar. Here all the
facing stones have been
robbed, leaving only the
infill

(KP)

Figure 3.8 (above right)
A length of town wall on
The Quay. The lowest four
courses of ragstone are
in their original position;
the rest has been repaired
and rebuilt

(EH NMR DP068610)

A few other pieces of town wall survive, some in the back gardens of houses along Strand Street and even in the cellar of the Bell Hotel (Figure 3.7) but they have all been restored and patched with rubble stones so that the their original appearance has been lost (Figure 3.8). The central stretch of the river frontage was never defended by a stone wall. This was not unusual in medieval ports where much of the riverbank was lined with private wharfs, not with quaysides belonging to the town. The merchants who owned them demanded a clear passage to their own space, where their cargoes could be loaded and unloaded. Town walls would have obstructed the course of business. In Sandwich, there was no riverside wall from the place where The Barbican now stands modernized where the Guestling joins the Stour.

The Black Death

At the end of the first decade of the war, another disaster struck the country. This was the Black Death (bubonic plague) which was at its height in England and continental Europe between 1348 and 1350, although there were sporadic outbreaks of it until the 1660s when the Great Plague of London of 1665–6 was its last devastating visit. During the first epidemic in 1348–9 up to half the population of England died, and Sandwich almost certainly suffered a similar fate with its population dropping from about 5,000 before the plague to about 2,500. There is little detailed information for the town

Figure 3.9 Interior of the chapel under the south-east corner of St Peter's church, probably used as a charnel house during the Black Death
(EH NMR DP032242)

but plague filled the old cemetery at St Clement's church, and there was a charnel house in St Peter's (Figure 3.9) for the bones of its parishioners. There was another severe outbreak in 1361, and several more during the next century. The most notable from Sandwich's point of view was the 1457 epidemic which so debilitated the leading citizens that the town was not in a position to defend itself when the French attacked in that year (see below page 89).

The Black Death must have left the town not only with many fewer inhabitants, but also a huge stock of unoccupied houses, many of which were probably left to abandonment and decay. It was not until the population began to increase again well on into the next century that new dwellings were needed and built. Most of the medieval houses that are still standing in Sandwich date from that time or slightly later, as we shall see in Chapter 4.

Sandwich people

The people about whom we know most are men who are mentioned in official documents of the time, mainly wealthy freemen who were eligible to become jurats, and to elect a mayor from among themselves. The jurats also chose two of their number to represent Sandwich at Westminster whenever a parliament was summoned. From the accession of Edward III in 1327 parliament met almost every year. New MPs were chosen for each parliament, but some served for many terms. They may have been the dominant forces within Sandwich's council of jurats, and during the years from 1368 to the end of the century they were drawn from only ten families, including the Condys, the Godards and the Elyses. The list of mayors shows a similar bias. In the same period we have the names of mayors for nineteen of the years; almost without exception, the same names occur. These families had a stranglehold on the town, which was exacerbated by some of them also holding positions of trust from the Crown, such as bailiff or Collector of Customs. Such posts helped to increase their families' wealth and status.

The families that dominated Sandwich society during the 14th century differed from those that we know of in the previous century, who mainly lived at the west end of town near the Priory buildings. Many of the new families lived further east, closer to what was becoming the commercial centre around Fishmarket, some of them in newly-built timber-framed houses in Strand Street and others in the streets slightly away from the busy waterfront. St Peter's rather than St Mary's may have become the dominant parish church, but the latter still benefited from donations and bequests from wealthy townspeople.

The Condy family is an example of the new 14th-century elite. The first time its name is mentioned is in 1310, when William Condy was mayor. To have reached such a position he must have been a jurat, and therefore a person of some standing for many years, probably back into the previous century. He had, moreover, started to build a dynasty, for his son John continued in public office, being elected mayor in 1326 and 1338. In 1326 John was master of the ship *La Godbiete*, of more than 50 tuns burden and manned by 40 mariners, which was forced to serve in the Scottish wars, and perhaps it was the same vessel that he captained in 1340 when it took part in the battle of Sluys. King Edward III recognized John's valour by making him bailiff of Sandwich; his son William took over the office on his death in 1345, serving as bailiff for nine years, and afterwards as Controller of Customs. The Condys continued to prosper; William's son or grandson John still imported luxury foodstuffs, such as the figs and raisins that he sold to the Priory in 1390. By the end of the century the family owned country property near Wingham and Eastry as well as houses and land all over Sandwich. Dynasty building still continued, for in 1399 Stephen Condy acquired a property in the High Street which was earmarked for his heirs. The dynasty did not last much longer though, for the last Condy to serve his home town was Lawrence, who was a Member of Parliament in 1420. However, we hear of one more Condy before they disappear from the records: Stephen, perhaps the son of the Stephen who bought property in High Street for his heirs. This Stephen was altogether more disreputable and in 1424 he was the leader of a group of mariners who boarded a ship in the Thames estuary, assaulted the crew and stole the cargo. Unfortunately for him, the cargo belonged to Master John Walewayn, the king's clerk, who had enough influence to prosecute a successful case against Condy and his crew. Nothing more is known about the family after that, but it certainly went out with a bang.

Some of the Condys had a spiritual side. When John the bailiff died in 1345 he bequeathed £4 to St Mary's church, to found a chantry where masses were to be said for his soul, and in 1377 Richard Condy, who owned a house in King Street, was a chaplain. Other families also gave generously to all three churches, although the gifts to St Mary's are the best known thanks to a surviving list of early benefactors and their bequests to the church. This list, known as a bede roll, was a call to the parishioners to pray for the souls of those who had embellished and improved the church over the years. Preserved only by chance, because such things were mostly destroyed at the Reformation, St Mary's bede roll starts with John and William Condy who founded and then maintained the chantry mentioned above. The next is Thomas Loveryk who paid for the construction of a Lady Chapel and three windows in the north aisle (Figures 3.10A & 3.10B). Then Harry Loveryk is mentioned. He gave a silver gilt monstrance in which the holy sacrament could be displayed when carried in procession on the day of Corpus Christi (the Thursday after Trinity Sunday, which is a week after Whit Sunday).

Thomas and Harry Loveryk were members of one of the richest of Sandwich's merchant families, who must already have been prosperous by about 1300. Later in the century, the Loveryks made good money out of the Hundred Years' War. For instance, in 1340 when the royal fleet that was about to set

Figure 3.10B One of the windows in the north aisle of St Mary's church, paid for by Thomas Loveryk in the 14th century

(HC)

out for Sluys it was found to be over-provisioned with foodstuffs such as flour and salt fish. John, William and Richard Loveryk bought the surplus at a rock-bottom price and then sold it to the townspeople at a profit. There is a suggestion of 'insider dealing' here, for one of the Loveryks' collaborators in the deal was John Condy, who was himself to sail with the fleet, and as a ship's master must have had prior knowledge of the state of the commissariat. Dubious commercial dealings are evidently not confined to the present day. John Loveryk must have been a jurat at the time of this business as he was mayor in 1355, but as we shall see, mayors could even be pirates without censure, so perhaps we should not be shocked at simple profiteering. Thomas Loveryk, one of the merchants who profited from the deal, was elected by his fellow jurats as a Member of Parliament for Sandwich. So he must have been considered a suitable candidate by the town's ruling body, many of whom may have envied his eye for a bargain.

St Mary's bede roll mentions John Godard 'of this parish' twice. His gifts to the church included a white damask cope embroidered in gold, a book on the lives of the martyrs and another (a *grayell*) containing music to be sung during the mass. Godard was a man of influence, being MP six times and mayor eleven times between 1376 and 1406. He was also Controller and Collector of Customs and held other Crown posts which must have brought him great wealth. All this was in addition to the £20 a year which he made from renting and leasing his properties outside the town.

The final dynasty that we have details for is the Elys family, whose most prominent member was Sir Thomas, who died in 1390 and left money for founding the third of Sandwich's medieval hospitals.

The Elyses may have begun as country gentry, for they are first heard of as landowners in the countryside around Wingham. They must have moved into Sandwich in the early decades of the 14th century, because by 1360 Thomas Elys, a draper, was able to make a substantial donation to St John's hospital. He was certainly a jurat by then, for he was elected mayor in 1370, when he was also Member of Parliament for Sandwich. His son, Sir Thomas, did not follow in his father's footsteps as a draper but improved his social standing by becoming a vintner who earned a good living by supplying wine to Christ Church Priory, and by serving as Collector of Customs. In 1377 he represented the town in the first parliament of Richard II's reign, and was mayor in 1382. During his lifetime he and his wife Margaret gave money for the construction and upkeep of the great west window in St Mary's church, but he chose to be buried in St Peter's churchyard, next to his father. He also established a chantry in St Peter's church, leaving a considerable sum for employing three priests to celebrate masses for his soul forever.

Sir Thomas made many other bequests, including a house in Love Lane for the three chantry priests and money for resurfacing the Cornmarket (Cattle Market) and for repairing roads and a bridge over the Delf. His greatest gift, though, was to endow a new hospital dedicated to St Thomas Becket, for eight men and four women. This added significantly to the provision for the poor of the town. The medieval hospital stood on a large plot of land between New Street and the Cornmarket and consisted of a great hall with eight rooms for the male inhabitants on its north side and four rooms for women on the south (Figure 3.11). Most of the buildings were demolished in 1857–8 when the new St Thomas's almshouses were built in Moat Sole but a few fragments survive. The south-east corner still stands in its original position, now forming part of the party wall between 14 and 16–18 New Street. The hall window, which can be seen in Figure 3.11, has been re-erected in St Peter's churchyard (Figure 3.12), and the porch is still in use as the entrance to the new almshouses (Figure 3.13).

The grandeur of the surviving early 14th-century houses in Strand Street show that it was a popular location for wealthy merchants to live but Sir Thomas, who may well have been the wealthiest of all, did not live there. His house and grounds were in Harnet Street. Now numbered as 29, it looks like an 18th-century brick building from the front, but the facade conceals a 16th-century wing against the street and, further back, the remains of the building that Elys would have occupied: a late 14th-century domestic wing,

Figure 3.11 The great hall of St Thomas's Hospital drawn by H. W. Rolfe in 1852

Figure 3.12 The window shown in Figure 3.11, re-erected in the churchyard at the west end of St Peter's church
(JT)

Figure 3.13 St Thomas's Hospital rebuilt in Moat Sole, with entrance porch on right
(JT)

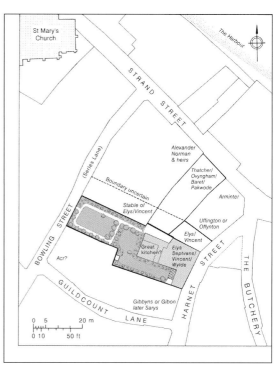

a great kitchen, and the site of a hall (Figures 3.14A & B). A deep but now blocked-up wine cellar underlines the fact that Elys was a vintner. Elys's house and grounds stood in a prime position not far from St Mary's church. His property stretched from Harnet Street to Bowling Street, and was next to the splendid knapped-flint wall shown in Figure 2.6. Using house deeds and other documents it has been possible to track down the names of some of Elys's neighbours (see Figure 3.14B). They were all prosperous merchants who made their money by shipping wine, cloth and grain, who served as jurats, mayors and MPs, and whose families inter-married to form inextricably connected dynasties. They and their descendants made up Sandwich's ruling class for the next fifty years or so, until the social and economic conditions changed.

Figure 3.14A (left)
The elegant Georgian front on Elys's house, now 29 Harnet Street
(GC)

Figure 3.14B (right)
The location of Elys's 14th-century house and its neighbours
(ATA)

Piracy and respectability

Almost as soon as the unofficial association of Cinque Ports came into being in the 11th century, the Portsmen who manned the ships belonging to the towns became renowned for their skill in seamanship, but also for their riotous and lawless behaviour, and piracy was one of their specialities. During the frequent periods of war with France piracy was totally acceptable, even encouraged, as the taking of foreign vessels could be said to help the war effort by capturing the 'king's enemies'. The cargoes were shared out among the crew as legitimate prizes won from the enemy. The trouble was that this behaviour often spilled over into peacetime, and great vessels laden with luxury goods frequently proved impossible to resist. Sandwich men were among the worst offenders.

Sometimes the piratical activities caused international diplomatic incidents. In 1320, for instance, a ship which set off from London with wool worth the considerable sum of 500 marks (many thousands of pounds in today's money) got no further than Sheppey when it was boarded by Robert Six of Sandwich and his associates who helped themselves to the wool. Unfortunately for the pirates, the owners of the cargo were Italian merchants, members of the influential Society of Peruzzi of Florence, who were well in with the king. They took their complaint to Edward II, and the case was still rumbling on four years later. On another occasion, Sancho the king of Majorca complained in that two of his country's galleys which had been loaded in English ports with 'cloth, wool, skins, silver, copper, tin and other merchandise' were set upon by men from the Cinque Ports. The spoils were then taken to Sandwich and divided among the Portsmen. The English were not the only culprits, though, nor yet the most daring. In 1323 French sailors audaciously captured a 'great ship called Dromundus' which lay at anchor in the calm waters of the Downs near Sandwich, carrying off its cargo worth £5,716 (a hefty six-figure sum today). This was a huge and profitable haul, but some other loot that the pirates brought home may have disappointed them, such as when a vessel from Groningen in The Netherlands was captured only to be found to contain a cargo of pitch.

Being accused, or even convicted, of piracy did not seem to carry any particular stigma. The best example of this comes from the 15th century when John Grene was accused, with others from Sandwich, of seizing a Flemish ship riding at anchor in the harbour at Plymouth. He and his companions were vilified as 'pirates and malefactors', yet he was mayor of Sandwich at the time (1430) and he also served as MP for the town on six occasions. By 1453 he confirmed, or perhaps bought, respectability in after life by establishing a chantry in St Clement's church.

Timeline 4

Sandwich		General	Reigns	
The Bulwark built	1451		1422–1461	Henry VI
Economic decline, but Calais still to be supplied by English ships, often from Sandwich	1453	End of Hundred Years' War, Calais remains in English hands		
Sandown Gate & New Gates first mentioned	1456			
	1455–85	Wars of the Roses		
French attack. Mayor John Drury killed	1457		1461–83	Edward IV
Davis Gate (Barbican) built in stone	1467			
Canterbury Gate & Woodnesborough Gate first mentioned	1468			
Last murage grant	1483		1483	Edward V
Town takes responsibility for castle	1483			
			1483–85	Richard III
		End of Wars of Roses	1485–1509	Henry VII
Petitions to Crown about Haven	1484, 1487			
War fleet assembled in Haven	1512	Henry VIII's expedition to France	1509–47	Henry VIII
Henry VIII in Sandwich en route to Dover	1532			
	1534	Reformation (Act of Supremacy)		
	1536–41	Dissolution of Monasteries		
Admiralty enquiry about Haven	1537			
Last mention of castle	1537			
Carmelite friary dissolved	1538			
Henry VIII visited Sandwich	1539			
Petition to king about harbour	1541			
Scheme for building new harbour	1548		1547–53	Edward VI
			1553–58	Mary I
Low point of economy	1558	Calais lost to English		
Petition to Crown about harbour	1561		1558–1603	Elizabeth I
Arrival of cloth workers from Low Countries, known as 'Strangers'; boost to town's economy	1561			
Manwood School founded & built	1563, 1564			
Elizabeth I visited Sandwich	1572			
Strangers outnumber native inhabitants, ill-feeling engendered	1574			
New Court Hall (Guildhall) built	1579			
Some Strangers leave for London or Norwich	1580s			
	1588	Spanish Armada		
Remaining Strangers claimed that they were too poor to pay taxes	1598			
Strangers gradually move elsewhere	early 1600s			

Developments in Sandwich c.1450–c.1600 set against major events in the history of England

4 The end of the Middle Ages: *c.*1450 to *c.*1600

The 15th and 16th centuries are characterized by an even greater increase and diversity in the sources of evidence. Records generated by the Crown's bureaucracy proliferated, and were bulked up by civic documents. The Town Council began to keep records of its meetings in minute books known as Town Year Books; the first to have been preserved dates from 1432. They are full of insights into the running of the town and the activities of its administration. What they tell us about life in Sandwich is made more real to us today through the many visible remains from the time. The picturesque dwelling houses and inns which line the streets, and The Barbican, the beautiful stone gateway that stands beside The Quay, are still preserved as mementos of the 15th- and 16th-century town.

This chapter will present some aspects of the town, drawn from information in the Year Books and from observations of the buildings. Sometimes we shall stray into the more recent past, but the history of modern Sandwich will not be found here. That still remains to be written by others.

Sandwich suffered many ups and downs during these years. At the beginning of the 15th century it was still recovering from the repercussions of the Black Death, which had left it with a greatly diminished population, empty houses and tracts of dereliction. Nevertheless, it managed to benefit from its position as a transit point for troops and provisions for the Hundred Years' War, and also during periods of peace great ships from Venice and Genoa visited the port with cargoes of wine, taking away cloth in return. The population gradually grew from its low point after the Black Death until there were about 3,500 people by the 1470s, and many of the houses that survive today were built at this time. The good times were not to last, however, as disease devastated the town and countryside and the Haven gradually silted up, becoming inaccessible to the Italian merchantmen so that they ceased to visit by the end of the century.

The early years of the 16th century were particularly hard, although there must have been a hint of the old days in 1512 when Henry VIII's war fleet assembled in the Haven for his expedition to France. By then Sandwich's population had again dropped to below 3,000, and it continued to go down for the next fifty years, when it received a boost with the arrival of the 'Strangers', religious refugees from The Netherlands (see page 91). By 1580 there were about 5,500 people living in the town, more than at any time before or since.

Houses

Almost 80 houses in the historic core of Sandwich survive from this period and virtually every street in the town has at least one house which is anything from 600 to 400 years old. Some streets have many more than one. In Strand Street, for instance, seventeen of its houses were built between the middle of the 15th century and c.1600 (Figure 4.1). In contrast, there is only one old house in Loop Street (Figure 4.2), perhaps not surprisingly, as that street was very much on the edge of the medieval town and never densely occupied.

Sandwich has kept so many of its old houses because in all periods land communications were poor, and once the Haven was no longer used by large vessels the town became an isolated backwater. There was no bridge across the river Stour until 1755, and the roads of East Kent were notoriously bad. So the town remained pretty well cut off from external influences until the end of the 18th century when turnpike roads were built. They linked into a road network which covered Kent and stretched even further afield, with regular stage-coach and carting service. Visitors came down from London,

Figure 4.1 This aerial view of Numbers 3–41 Strand Street shows the full extent of this street of medieval houses, the longest continuous row of timber-framed buildings to survive in any English town
(EH NMR 24073/20)

primarily to the newly popular sea-bathing resorts of the Thanet coast, but some found their way to Sandwich. They brought a modest prosperity to the town and with it a desire to modernize on the part of the people who lived there. Following the example set by the councillors of Canterbury, most of the medieval town gates were demolished to improve traffic flow, and it was proposed that part of St Mary's church should be knocked down to widen Strand Street when that stretch of the street was straightened in the 'modernization'. In the event, just the north-east corner of the church was trimmed off (Figure 4.3).

At the same time, many townspeople brought their 15th- or 16th- century timber-framed houses up to date. The most expensive and drastic approach, to rebuild entirely, was taken by a few of the wealthier inhabitants, some of whom lived in the comparatively wide and spacious High Street where there are now several genuine Georgian houses (Figure 4.4). For the rest, the houses

Figure 4.2 (above)
The Old Cottage, the only 15th-century house in Loop Street
(JT)

Figure 4.3 (right)
The north-east corner of St Mary's church against Strand Street, trimmed in the 18th century
(HC)

Figure 4.4 (below)
Aerial view of the east side of High Street, with grand Georgian houses in the centre
(EH NMR 24064/17)

Figure 4.5 East side of St Peter's Street which now shows predominantly flat-fronted brick houses which hide their medieval origins

(GC)

simply had 'face lifts'. A popular thing to do was to cut back the jetties (the upper overhanging storeys on the front of a building) and to add a 'modern' facade with large windows. As a result the narrow medieval streets became lined with buildings with the flat, brick or stucco fronts that still make up much of the townscape of today (Figure 4.5). In some, mundane materials were used to produce very exotic effects (see Figure 2.5A). The Middle Ages are present in the narrowness of most of the streets and the absence of high-rise buildings. There are not many medieval structures above three storeys, and the remarkably few tall buildings from the 18th and 19th centuries stand out as something unusual.

The town plan has changed hardly at all in recent centuries; even the coming of the railway in 1847 did little to affect it. The streets and the houses beside them proved sufficient to accommodate the population, which is now little more than when the ramparts were built in the early 14th century to defend the town and also to define its boundary. Then the population was at its medieval maximum, living in perhaps 1,000 houses, tightly packed beside the narrow streets. Although the population has fluctuated over the centuries it has only recently exceeded 5,000, and so there has been no need for new houses along new streets. Today there are 928 households in the historic core of the town, generally living beside the same medieval streets. Six new closes or cul-de-sacs have been laid out in recent years, but the overall street pattern is as it was 600 years ago.

Domestic arrangements

Until the late years of the 16th century, living conditions in the houses cannot have been very much more comfortable than in earlier years. In some, there was still a high hall open to the rafters, which served as a formal entrance and entertaining space in the grander houses. In smaller dwellings it was still the centre of domestic activities, and in both cases it was usually still the only heated room in the house. In the commercial centre of the town, where there was pressure on land, houses were arranged so that their gables faced the street. In those, the hall was in the middle of the house, with rooms on two or more storeys to the front and back. Figure 4.6 shows a simple outline of this arrangement. Further away from the town centre the plots of land on which the houses stood were often wider, and so the hall was placed parallel to the street, and the additional rooms were at the side. In both cases, some of the rooms flanking the hall may have been used as shops or warehouses, not necessarily as living space. Until the middle of the 16th century most rooms seem to have served many purposes, with one dedicated to sitting, eating, entertaining or sleeping being an innovation.

We know more about living conditions after the middle of the 16th century when some inventories of household goods survive. They show that by

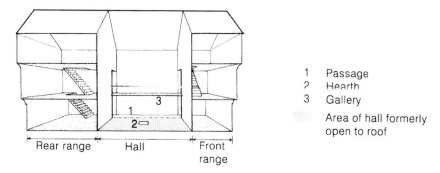

Figure 4.6 Schematic drawing of a 15th-century house with an open hall crossed by a gallery
(ATA)

1 Passage
2 Hearth
3 Gallery
Area of hall formerly open to roof

Figure 4.7 (left)
An example of an
Elizabethan building:
Manwood House built as
a grammar school in 1564
(EH NMR DP0433948)

Figure 4.8 (opposite)
Strand Street looking east
(JT)

then the richer classes of society lived in houses with many rooms on several floors. In general, the halls were used as reception rooms with all cooking relegated to kitchens, and there were sitting rooms (parlours), and bedrooms. They could be well furnished, with textile hangings on the walls to keep out draughts and fireplaces with brick-built chimney stacks to carry away the smoke. In addition to the tables and benches of earlier centuries, there were wooden chairs, cupboards in which eating equipment, silverware or household linen could be kept, curtains and cushions, and even wooden bedsteads in bed chambers.

The less well-off lived in smaller houses with fewer rooms, so there was no possibility for them to indulge in such a lifestyle. They kept to a more old-fashioned way of life, with their rooms still serving many purposes.

Some streetscapes

Although many of the medieval houses are now hidden behind 18th- and 19th-century fronts, most of the Sandwich streets have some houses which still show their origins, either with visible framing or jettied upper stories.

Figure 4.9 Air view of
Strand Street showing
the King's Lodging (1),
St Mary's church (2), the
Kings Arms (3), Guestling
Mill (4) and the Long
House (5)
(EH NMR 24064/11)

Strand Street has houses of all periods, from the early 14th century (Figure 3.1A) to Elizabethan. The timber-framed houses on the south side, such as those in Figure 4.8, are reminders of the streets commercial origins, with the tall gable at the far end having been a tavern and others being shops. The aerial view on Figure 4.9 shows the King's Lodging (1), St Mary's church (2), the Kings Arms of 1592 (3), and the Long House built in the 1560s (5). The most recent building is Guestling Mill, founded as a brewery in the 19th century (4). Church Street St Mary,

Figure 4.10 Church Street St Mary, lined by mainly 16th-century houses

(HC)

which joins Strand Street at the church, is another very picturesque street (Fig. 4.10), with houses mostly dating from the late 16th and early 17th centuries. They still have their jetties and in several cases their timbers are visible.

Upper Strand Street appears to be a total contrast to Strand Street, and yet the two were regarded as one until the late 19th century, when 'Upper' was added to its name. It has a much more modern feel about it than Strand Street but it is actually older in origin. It lies on the Thanet Beds, whereas Strand Street is partly on Alluvium and partly on ground that had been reclaimed from the river (see Figures 1.7C & 1.8). Numbers 15–25 on the north side of Upper Strand Street (Figure 4.11) and 22–24 and 32–34 on the south side (overleaf) all date from the 15th or early 16th centuries and most of their external medieval features have been removed but there are a few visible remains of medieval timber framing, for example at the corner of Quay Lane where the end wall of Number 19 Upper Strand Street shows its structure (Figure 4.12).

Figure 4.11 Numbers 15–25 Upper Strand Street. The timber-framed houses have been modernized by having their fronts cut back (GC)

Figure 4.12 Timber framing visible on the west wall of Number 19 Upper Strand Street (GC)

High Street was called Guild-hall Street until the middle of the 15th century. There was a guildhall there in the 13th century, but we do not know whether it was the headquarters of a trade guild, a religious guild or for the town. The town's present Town Hall in the Cattle Market is called the Guildhall, but in earlier centuries the name Court Hall was used to describe where the town's business was carried on. High Street's real importance before the middle of the 14th century was in its crucial position in communications between town and hinterland. The highway from the south ran along High Street towards the ferry across the Stour which was the only means of reaching Thanet from Sandwich until the toll bridge was built in the middle of the 18th century (see Figure 2.1). The widest part of the street served as a market place, but its importance faded once the original southern entrance into town was blocked by Mill Wall and as Cornmarket flourished. However, it remained as the place where the annual St Clement's fair was held until the late 19th century. Before the 14th century the houses in High Street were large and grand as is shown by Number 20 (see Figure 2.5A), but once the market declined it was lined by much smaller timber-framed dwellings. It regained its prominence in the late 18th and early 19th centuries when it was greatly favoured by the professional classes who probably appreciated its layout; it is wider and straighter than many other streets in the town. They also demanded more spacious accommodation than that provided by the small 15th-century dwellings that stood there. So many of them were totally rebuilt in the up-to-the-minute style rather than being refaced as they were in other parts of the town (this is shown well by the aerial view in Figure 4.4). The result is a pleasant mixture of big brick houses and smaller ones with timber framing, bricks and stucco (Figures 4.14A & 4.14B).

Figure 4.13   Numbers 32–34 Upper Strand Street. The early 16th-century house is now disguised by an 18th-century brick exterior
(JT)

*Figure 4.14A The west
side of High Street,
looking north*

(JT)

High Street, Sandwich

*Figure 4.14B The same
view in 1906*

(SGA PC01-276E)

Figure 4.17 The jetties had been cut back by the time this photo was taken
(SGA: BVP-00014)

Figure 4.18 Number 7 Market Street with its jettied front cut back and covered in mathematical tiles
(JT)

Market Street, called Fishmarket from the earliest years of the town, fairly successfully hides its medieval origins, and so is a prime example of how medieval buildings can be modernized. Numbers 4–10 Market Street were built in the 15th century, as the steep pitches of the roofs show (Figure 4.15). The houses were still more or less intact in 1792 when Figure 4.16 was published, but the jetties had been cut back by the time the photograph was taken a century later (Figure 4.17). A different type of modernization can be seen opposite in Number 7 (Figure 4.18), which was also built in the 15th century. When its jetties were removed in the 18th century it became ultra-modern by having its front covered in mathematical tiles, an ingenious type of tile imitating brick. These tiles are unusual in Sandwich, but another building clad in them can be seen on the front of St Peter's vicarage in King Street. They were manufactured and used for only a short period, so they are a good indicator of 18th-century modifications.

4.19 (left) Air view of the medieval Cornmarket with the Guildhall on the west side   (EH NMR 24084/23)

4.20 (above) The right-hand end of the Guildhall was built in 1579. It is still used as a Coroner's Court and Town Council offices   (JT)

Cattle Market (medieval Cornmarket) was the third of Sandwich's market places, founded in the 13th century (Figure 4.19). Today it is dominated by the Guildhall (Figure 4.20) which was built in 1579 as the town's administrative centre or Court Hall. That building is still the core of the present one, which has been added to over the centuries, until it achieved its present appearance in 1973. When first built it had a court room on the ground floor, and a council chamber and treasury above. The Town Council still meets in the council chamber, and the court room, still with much of its original furniture, is used as a Coroner's Court. The court room is open to the public, and well worth a visit. Appropriately, the streets around the Cattle Market contain some old commercial buildings, notably the curiously named No Name Shop in No Name Street. It was built in the 15th century to house four tiny shops and a smithy (Figures 4.21 & 4.22).

There are other streets where the demands of modern commerce happily co-exist with the medieval past. King Street, for example, is now one of the economic hubs of Sandwich, with shops along much of its length. Some were built as shops in the 15th century others in the 19th century (Figure 4.23). This ability to merge old and new can been seen throughout the town.

More details of streetscapes and individual houses can be found in *Walks through Historic Sandwich*, published in 2011.

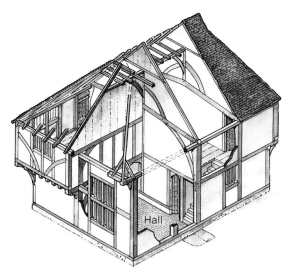

Hall

First floor

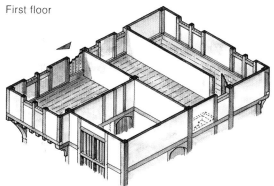

Ground floor

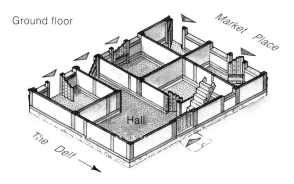

Market Place

Hall

The Delf

Figure 4.21 (above) The No Name Shop today. The Delf flows beside it, hidden by the brick wall, and the 19th-century pump still stand there
(JT)

Figure 4.22 (left) The layout of No Name Shop when it was first built
(ATA)

THE CORNER HOUSE

Figure 4.23 A 19th-century shop at the junction of King Street (left) and St Peter's Street
(JT)

Sandwich people: merchants

In the early years of the 15th century the wealthy merchants continued their custom of living near to each other, socializing, and intermarrying. William Gayler is typical of these. He was a very rich man and mayor of Sandwich five times between 1417 and 1427. He and his wife Elizabeth were parishioners of St Mary's, with properties in Love Lane and Strand Street, including a riverside tenement near the church, where he had his own private quay and crane, the marks of a wealthy merchant. True to form, when Elizabeth remarried shortly after William's death, it was to another rich merchant, Robert Whyte, mayor from 1433 to 1435. Whyte already had a daughter when he married Elizabeth as his second wife, and on coming of age in 1439 her father gave her three properties: one in Strand Street and two in High Street. The one in Strand Street was in what sounds a not very salubrious position as it was opposite the lane to the common privy beside Davis Gate (now called The Barbican). This may be reflected in its annual rent of only 8s. Nevertheless, its tenant then was Henry Cok, a member of a family which was an important part of the Sandwich elite throughout the 15th century.

The Coks first came to prominence in 1423 when Henry was mayor. He was mayor again in 1426 and MP in 1428 and 1429. It is difficult to imagine a man of such eminence living near to the common privy, but this may be bringing a 21st-century view to a medieval matter. Between 1440 and 1458 Richard Cok continued the tradition of serving the town as mayor and MP, and he may have grown wealthier than his father, for he moved from being a tenant near the privy to become a property owner near Fisher Gate, probably next to Quay Lane. His house fronted onto Upper Strand Street, with the land behind it running down to the river bank where there was a private wharf. He was followed in public office by his sons John, Robert and William, with William still living in the Upper Strand Street house, which may be the house which still stands on the corner of Quay Lane (see Figure 4.12).

Henry Cok and his kin seem to have made their money as merchants dealing in goods from abroad, the wharf suggesting that waterborne trade was their speciality. But by the middle of the 15th century local traders and craftsmen rather than international merchants were coming to prominence in the town. There were at least two reasons for this. In the 1450s the town changed from being governed solely by a mayor and jurats (in effect by a small coterie of rich merchants) to having another tier of government, the 'common council', in which less affluent townsmen could serve. At the same time, long-distance trade was becoming less important to the town, so there were fewer and fewer wealthy merchants.

Sandwich people: tradesmen

The general traders, craftsmen and artisans who gradually took over from the merchants continued the tradition of civic service, and also of marrying within their own small circle so that most of the influential people in the town were related in one way or another. This is illustrated by the Boteler family of drapers and barbers, who worked both in Sandwich and in the English possession of Calais. The founder of the dynasty was John, a draper who lived in Strand Street in a house with shops on the street frontage. He was mayor four times and MP twice between 1439 and 1447. He was succeeded by his sons, Richard and John, who inherited his property, and by his nephew Thomas who was prosperous enough to buy his own house next to Pillory Gate. The family name died out at the beginning of the 16th century when there were no further male heirs. The Boteler properties were then sold off, with several being bought by Roger Manwood who was also a draper. He must have been a friend of, if not related to, the Botelers. At the time of the sale in 1514 Roger was already a substantial merchant, having been a jurat for some time. He was later elected mayor for two terms of office and also served as an MP. His descendants dominated Sandwich government and society in the 16th century, so much so that one (Sir Roger, who held high office in the Court of Elizabeth I) founded a school for boys of the town in 1563 and entertained Queen Elizabeth when she visited Sandwich in 1572. The school in Strand Street is now private domestic accommodation but there is still a Sir Roger Manwood Grammar School on the outskirts of the town. The house where Queen Elizabeth slept (and Henry VIII slept before her) was demolished long ago, although its name the 'King's Lodging' is now given to 46 Strand Street.

Drapers seem to have been particularly successful in the 15th and 16th centuries, but men following other trades also grew rich and influential enough to become jurats, mayors, or MPs. Brewers, for instance, were among the wealthiest people in the town from the second half of the 15th century as a result of the change from brewing ale to brewing beer and the beginning of large-scale beer production. Brewing beer involves using hops, which give it a characteristic bitter flavour and, more importantly, act as a preservative. So hopped beer could be kept for much longer than ale, which until then had been the drink of choice for most social classes.

Sandwich people: beer brewers, inns and taverns

Hopped beer was first introduced into England from The Netherlands so it is no surprise that it was foreigners who first brewed it in Sandwich, starting in 1439. The next brewers that we hear of were natives of Sandwich, implying that the Netherland monopoly had been broken, and by the 1470s Cornelius Beerbrewer and William Giles, both Englishmen, were as rich as anyone in the town. Giles's brewery stood between Strand Street and the river, near its junction with Bowling Street where he also had stables and storehouses. A building on the north side of Strand Street with the modern name plate 'Giles Quay' probably marks the site of his brewery (see Figure 4.26).

Much of the beer produced by the Sandwich brewers went to provision ships, but it was also sold in the local inns and taverns. Today, the Crispin Inn and the Admiral Owen facing each other at the east end of Strand Street (Figure 4.24). The Kings Arms at the corner of Church Street St Mary, and the George and Dragon in Fisher Street (Figure 4.25) are all traditional pubs with old-fashioned interiors. They may not have been built as inns in the Middle Ages, but they give a good impression of having been so.

For the rest, we mostly know their names and locations from written sources, but some, such as the New Tavern at the corner of Harnet Street, survived long enough to be photographed (Figure 5.2B). And one other still stands, but in a very different guise. This is 46 Strand Street (Figure 4.26), which had been built as a merchant's house in the 15th century and then enlarged a hundred years later when it was probably converted into the White Hart inn. It stands opposite Bowling Street, named after the inn's bowling alley (see below). By the late 15th century it seems to have been good business to own an inn, not to be its working landlord but to hold it as property which could be leased out. Thomas Aldy was one such. His father John had been MP and mayor in the 1460s and 1470s, and by 1490 Thomas

Figure 4.24 The Admiral Owen and Crispin Inn at the east end of Strand Street

(GC)

Figure 4.25 The George and Dragon in Fisher Street

(HC)

Figure 4.26 The King's Lodging from the air. Built in the 15th century and probably converted into the White Hart Inn in the 16th century. The name plate 'Giles Quay' is on the wall of an adjacent building to the west.

(EH NMR 24073/26)

himself was mayor. In 1493 he owned the New Tavern, and by 1513 he was one of the richest men in the town.

Those inns were all privately owned, but there were three which were civic property. One of them was the Bull Inn. It seems to have occupied 11–15 Strand Street, a courtyard property originally built in the 13th and 14th centuries for a wealthy merchant, and partially rebuilt around 1500 (Figure 4.27). Figure 4.28 shows the remains of the archway of the carriage entrance to the yard. The Black Tavern was also owned by the town. It was probably where 27 Strand Street stands today (see Figure 4.8); this is a timber-framed house above a 14th-century stone cellar which may have been the licensed premises. The third civic property, the Bell Inn, stood on the west side of Love Lane but has left no remains. All three were used for official civic functions such as banquets for the mayor and his entourage, but they were also patronized by the public who used them not just as drinking establishments but also as places of entertainment, where music and even theatrical performances were sometimes put on for all.

Drinking, feasting, listening to music or watching plays were not the only things that happened in the inns and taverns. Many were notorious for the so-called 'unlawful games' – dice, cards, bowls, tennis and skittles – that

Figure 4.27 Number 13–15 Strand Street (with the sign board) was the Bull Inn in the 15th and 16th centuries
(JT)

Figure 4.28 Detail of the archway which once led from Strand Street into the courtyard of the inn
(JT)

were played in them. Bowling alleys, associated with the inns and therefore drinking establishments as well as gaming places, became particularly notorious because they were said to tempt servants away from their lawful occupations to places where they could drink, and very probably start brawling. Sandwich had at least one bowling alley as early as 1517. We know about it because the proprietor was fined for not stopping an affray on his premises. However, there is no evidence to suggest that the White Hart's bowling alley in Bowling Street was anything but respectable.

Bad behaviour of all kinds was frowned upon by the civic authorities, who attempted to quell it by all means possible. Women's sexual morals were a particular target. When a woman was accused of fornication or being a prostitute she was driven out of town, and things grew so bad that in 1465 nine women were exiled for their misdemeanours. The council's answer to the problem was to set up an official brothel which, it was hoped, would confine the problem to a designated part of the town. In 1474 John Kyng, a brewer, leased a barn and garden in St Clement's parish to the mayor and councillors for this purpose. It was either in Millwall Place, or Knightrider Street, both of which were rather insignificant cul-de-sacs near the town ramparts, and well away from the town centre. Sandwich was really rather brave in doing this. The only other places in medieval England where the civic authorities owned and ran brothels were Southampton and the London suburb of Southwark – both the haunt of mariners, as Sandwich must have been.

The decline of Sandwich Haven

Once the Hundred Years' War ended in 1453, Sandwich lost its naval and military importance, and hence much of its income. It needed to carry on the long-distance trade which had been its lifeline during the decades before the Hundred Years' War, but this was becoming impossible as the Haven was silting up and becoming inaccessible to the cargo vessels carrying goods from Genoa, Venice and Spain. By the 1460s the town council was growing more and more worried about the state of the Haven and the first of many petitions about digging out a new harbour was sent to the Crown. No help was forthcoming, and the situation became progressively worse. By the beginning of the 16th century, buoys were needed to mark the navigable channels through the sandbanks. The banks accumulated naturally, but

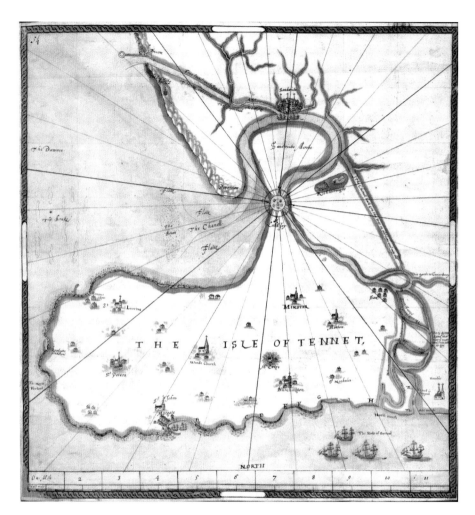

Figure 4.29 A chart of Sandwich Haven showing John Rogers's plans for a new channel to the coast. The orientation is the reverse of that used today as south is at the top. The tiny picture of Sandwich is the earliest known depiction of the town

were made much more treacherous by the ballast dumped into the Haven when visiting ships needed more cargo space.

By the end of the 1540s there had been several Admiralty enquiries and an abortive attempt to build a new harbour. John Rogers, a renowned military engineer who had supervised the harbour works at Calais, was commissioned for yet another Sandwich project. His plan was to dig an artificial channel from Sandwich Haven to the sea, as shown on a chart drawn at the time (Figure 4.29). Work started in 1548, but financial difficulties led to it being abandoned shortly after it had begun.

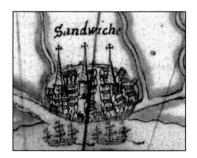

There were more petitions to royalty throughout the rest of the century. The mayor went to London in 1560 to petition Queen Elizabeth, and she was said to look favourably on the request, but nothing more happened until she visited Sandwich in 1572 when she was presented with a letter asking for help with the Haven. The mayor and jurats persisted, and in 1575 yet another proposal was submitted to the Crown. This time it was Andrian Andrison, an engineer, who drew up an impressive scheme, but its estimated cost of £13,000 meant that it was doomed to failure. By the 1620s the estimate had risen to £50,000, and it must finally have become obvious that the Haven could not be saved even with the expenditure of enormous sums of money.

In the 1740s a report on relocating the harbour from Sandwich to the coast near Sandown Castle was submitted to a Committee of the House of Commons. The work was to cost £389,168. 13s. 2d, not including the purchase of coastal land. The Committee's conclusions were enthusiastically in favour, specifically because a safe harbour near Sandown Castle could provide an anchorage for warships, and 'be of great use and advantage to the naval Power of Great Britain'. Sadly for Sandwich, this plan was abandoned, probably on grounds of cost, and when the question of an east coast port was raised again it was Ramsgate that was favoured over Sandwich. By the end of the 18th century between £600,000 and £700,000 had been spent to give Ramsgate a new, entirely man-made, harbour and to transform it from 'a place consisting of a few mean hovels' to a thriving port and seaside resort. In contrast, Sandwich continued to decline, used only by local traffic: lighters and barges carrying miscellaneous small cargoes. Until the early 20th century, barges were carrying coal as far upstream as Fordwich, and small craft can still negotiate their way from Pegwell Bay to the quayside at Sandwich. But the river Stour is hardly navigable west of Sandwich today.

The Barbican and other gates

The town defences, which had been begun in the 14th century, continued to be added to and improved. When the ramparts were first built there were no gates across the roads leading through them from the surrounding countryside. They were guarded by barriers across the roads, known as bars or turnpikes, which would not have provided much protection against determined attack. In 1435 the town decreed that the bars should be made

more defensible, and that was probably when they were converted into the gatehouses which stood around the town until the late 18th century (Figures 4.30–4.32). Three were drawn shortly before they were demolished, and it is largely thanks to those drawings that we know more or less what they looked like. Two of the quayside gateways survive: Fisher Gate built at the end of the 14th century (see Figure 3.6) and Davis Gate (now called The Barbican) built in its present form in the late 1460s (Figure 4.33). The reason for its present name is unclear. Almost as soon as the gatehouse was built there was a structure beside it called 'barbican' or 'barbican house', apparently used for storage. As late as 1776 a watch tower called The Barbican is said to have stood at one end of David's Gate. Now that name is applied to the gatehouse itself.

Although the present Barbican dates from the second half of the 15th century, Davis Quay was a landmark by 1301 when it is mentioned in the Custumal, and Davis Gate itself is recorded

Figure 4.30 Canterbury Gate in the late 18th century
(Boys *Collections*)

Figure 4.31 Woodnesborough Gate in the late 18th century
(Boys *Collections*)

Figure 4.32 Sandown Gate in the late 18th century
(Boys *Collections*)

from the early fourteenth century onwards. Its precise position at that date is unknown, but it stood at a strategic point, near the ferry to and from Thanet, and at the north end of the High Street. What can be seen today was begun in 1467, when Davy Dyker and his workmen dug foundations and sank piles into the river bed to prepare for the construction of a new Davis Gate. Three years later great quantities of ragstone, chalk, flint, hewn stone, sand and lime were brought from Folkestone for use in the superstructure, under the supervision of the mason Thomas Whyteler. All those materials are still visible in the gate today

The chequerwork decoration of alternating squares of flint and limestone (Figure 4.34) makes Davis Gate one of the most spectacular gates in any small town in England, and suggests that Davis Gate was put up partly as a status symbol, as a welcome but also a warning to those who came to Sandwich by sea. It was built at a cost of almost £200, a great sum in those days, and money continued to be spent on it for the next hundred years. The mayor and council were very proud of what became the symbol of their town. Nevertheless, Davis Gate had at least the pretence of being a defensive structure, for there are gun loops in the base of the towers, through which the guns purchased by the town in 1483 could have been fired (Figure 4.35).

Figure 4.33 (below)
The Barbican (originally Davis Gate) beside The Quay
(HC)

Figure 4.34 (right)
Detail of the decoration on the towers, a chequer pattern of flint and Caen stone
(HC)

Figure 4.35 (bottom right)
Gun loops, now blocked, in the basement of the east tower of The Barbican
(SP)

The Bulwark

By the middle of the century the town council must have become aware that the ramparts were insufficient to defend the town from attack from the sea and that they needed to be supplemented by artillery. So, in 1451 the north-east corner of the town was strengthened by a 'new wall for guns' which was gradually extended to become a fort known as The Bulwark. Part of the fort survives today as a continuation of the Mill Wall rampart, running from Sandown Road towards the river, but originally it was almost square, surrounded by walls and ditches which enclosed a two-storey tower used as an arsenal and with a great gun known as 'the Murderer' beside the entrance from the town. The ramparts that survive today are thick earth walls fronted by stone and brick in places and with a dry moat (originally Sandown Creek) in front of them (Figure 4.36). But these were only part of The Bulwark's defences, for when it was built the tidal waters of the river Stour flowed close to its northern side and also filled Sandown Creek to the east. Almost as soon as it was built the town was attacked by French forces who kept up intermittent raids on the English coast even though the Hundred Years' War was officially over.

Figure 4.36 The wall of The Bulwark against Sandown Creek
(HC)

This raid took place in August 1457, when the French overwhelmed The Bulwark and occupied the town during the hours of daylight, withdrawing only after both sides had suffered heavy losses. The attack is remembered by Sandwich people to this day as the time when their mayor, John Drury, was slain while gallantly defending his town. He is still mourned by the mayors of Sandwich, who wear a black, rather than a red, robe on civic occasions.

The Bulwark may have borne the brunt of the brief but deadly attack, for it seems to have been damaged quite badly, so much so that it was still being repaired twelve years later. It was then kept well defended for several centuries, and it was still maintained until it was demolished in the middle of the 18th century. By then it was an 'ancient tower, 20ft high, 30ft long and 20ft wide', topped by battlements and overlooking the harbour. In the early 20th century the land where The Bulwark had stood was transformed into the gardens of the Salutation, a mansion designed by Sir Edwin Lutyens in 1911 (Figure 4.37). The gardens have recently been restored according to

Figure 4.37 Air view of the Salutation with the Secret Gardens behind it, where the 15th-century Bulwark fort once stood

(EH NMR 24064/06)

The Bulwark

their original plan and can be visited as The Secret Gardens of Sandwich. Although the gardens are very beautiful, their landscaping has removed all traces of the once very substantial Bulwark.

The churches in the 15th and 16th centuries

During the 15th century St Clement's church reached its present appearance (see Figure 3.5). The nave was rebuilt and heightened, with pointed arches and a new roof of East Anglian type, decorated inside with angels (Figure 4.38). Another unusual feature can be seen at the east end where some 15th-century choir stalls stand on their original stone bases (Figure 4.39). The circular holes in the bases were cut to hold clay pots (known as acoustic jars) to improve acoustics. More holes in the wall above served the same purpose.

*Figure 4.38 (above)
One of the angels on the nave roof of St Clement's church*
(JT)

Figure 4.39 Wooden choir stalls from the 15th century standing on a base with holes which once held acoustic jars
(JT)

At the same time, St Mary's church was being embellished with a new tower and peal of bells. Caen stone was imported from Normandy and ragstone brought from Folkestone to build the tower, and a mason employed at Canterbury cathedral acted as a consultant. Despite the great care and expense involved in the building, the tower fell down in 1668, destroying most of the body of the church. Sandwich reputedly suffered an earthquake in 1597, and this may have damaged the foundations, so contributing to the fall. It may be no coincidence that St Peter's tower also collapsed in the 1660s.

At the Reformation all three parish churches had to change to the new faith, and St Peter's in particular became strongly protestant. All the priests married as soon as it was allowed, and when Queen Mary reinstated Catholicism there were no unmarried priests in the town. In 1564 St Peter's became the 'Dutch church', used solely by the Dutch-speaking Calvinist immigrants (Strangers, see below) who started arriving in Sandwich in 1561. It continued to serve them for more than 50 years, and after its tower fell down in 1661, descendants of the original Stranger congregation paid for it to be rebuilt.

The Strangers usher in a new era

In 1560 refugees fleeing from religious persecution in The Netherlands were encouraged to settle in England, and Sandwich welcomed them enthusiastically. At the time the town was suffering from a severe economic depression, and its population had sunk to an unprecedented low. Most of the Strangers were specialized cloth makers, manufacturing finer woollen cloth than was then known in England. Sandwich had long produced cloth on a small scale, but when the immigrants took over the industry became much more significant. French speaking Walloons soon came to join their Dutch speaking compatriots, and by 1574 they jointly outnumbered the locals. They also started to work at trades other than cloth making, and, not surprisingly, this led to friction between them and the native Sandwich inhabitants. The locals felt that their own jobs were under threat, and so the council proposed that the Strangers should be subject to certain restrictions; they could not, for instance, make shoes, tailor clothing or even bake bread without a licence.

The question also arose as to where the Strangers should live. Initially there was little difficulty as when the population was declining throughout the first half of the 16th century many houses, mainly on the outer edges of the town but still within the walled area, had been abandoned and left to decay. So there must have been a stock of empty houses. But once the number of Strangers started to increase, the situation changed and there was a great demand for housing. Some of the derelict properties must have been brought back into use and rented to the 159 foreign households that were in Sandwich by 1565. The empty houses were not enough though, so the Council encouraged the townspeople who could afford it to build houses on specific areas of vacant land near Canterbury Gate, along New Street and elsewhere on the fringes of the historic core. Many of the landlords of these new houses were merchants, most of them jurats

Figure 4.40 Number 7 Bowling Street, a grand house built in the late 16th century
(EH NMR DP032215)

and therefore part of the town elite who, already rich, became richer from their part in housing the Strangers, and this is reflected in the surviving architecture. Some of the new landlords built themselves large, up-to-the-minute dwellings such as 7 Bowling Street (Figure 4.40). Other houses were renovated, including 46 Strand Street (see Figure 4.26). With increasing prosperity came greater civic pride, for in 1579 a new Court Hall was opened in the Cornmarket (see Figure 4.20). Today this is called the Guildhall, and is Sandwich's Town Hall, housing the Museum and Tourist Information Office as well as the Council offices.

Most of the houses that were built to rent to the Strangers were in great contrast to those of their English landlords, being small and rather poorly built. Very few have escaped demolition, although a pair of semi-detached cottages at 6 and 8 Bowling Street (Figure 4.41) has fortunately survived. Small medieval houses were also divided up to accommodate Strangers,

with the two small houses of 17 and 19 High Street being good examples of what was once a single dwelling (Figure 4.42).

As early as the 1580s some of the Strangers left Sandwich to live in London or Norwich, where there were also immigrant communities, or to return to The Netherlands once the religious problems had been largely resolved. Those who were left behind may have been the poor who could not afford to travel, for in 1598 they complained to the Town Council that they were too poor to pay all of the local taxes. Nevertheless, more immigrants came to join them in the years after 1600, but by then the time when the Strangers changed the Sandwich economy and demography was long gone.

5 Postscript: the 500 years since the Strangers left town

Sandwich is now perceived to be an urban gem, a beautiful place to visit and a highly desirable place to live. But that has not always been the case. At the end of the 17th century the diarist Celia Fiennes obviously did not like it, and noted that it was 'a sad old town ... run so to Decay that Except one or two good houses its just like to Drop down ye whole town'. Seymour's survey of Kent compiled in the 1770s is slightly more complimentary. High Street, Fisher Street and Delf Street are said to be the 'broadest and most airy' with several good houses (Figure 5.1), probably built and occupied by some of the

Figure 5.1 Delph House in Delf Street, one of the 'good houses' referred to in the 18th century

(GC)

few wealthy merchants who also frequented the assembly room that had recently been laid out in the New Inn. That no longer exists, presumably swept away when the present New Inn was built (Figures 5.2A and B), but there is still an equivalent at the Bell Hotel (Figure 5.3). Seymour also criticized Strand Street, which many now regard as the highlight of the town, for it 'might have been a commodious thoroughfare but at present is broken into many disagreeable angles'. The same view was held right at the end of the 18th century when Edward Hasted published the first comprehensive history of Kent. He maintained that the houses were 'old-fashioned and ill built'. The streets were generally 'narrow and ill-convenient lanes, little adapted for carriages or even horses.' High Street was singled out as the exception, though, for it was 'of good breadth and much better built.' This is still true today, even down to the elegantly carved parish boundary marker set into a wall on its east side (Figures 5.4A and B).

Figure 5.3 The 18th-century assembly room at the New Inn was probably similar to that still surviving in the Bell Hotel above

(GC)

Figure 5.4A (left) The elegantly carved stone in High Street marking the boundary between the parishes of St Clement (S - C) and St Peter (S - P)

(GC)

Figure 5.4B (right) The less precisely carved boundary stone in Delf Street, between the parishes of St Peter and St Mary

(GC)

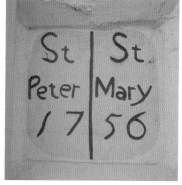

All these authors were reflecting the spirit of their age, for it was a time when timber-framed and jettied houses were looked upon as hovels. They might have been more positive in their opinion of Sandwich if they had visited it in the early years of the 19th century when many of the houses had been modernized. That was the time when brick and stucco facades were put in place, and large windows inserted. But some of the houses escaped that treatment and survived to become looked after and cherished by their owners today.

The surviving timber-framed houses have had their ups and downs, too. Sandwich Guildhall Archive has an excellent collection of photographs and picture postcards of the town in the early 20th century, showing the condition of buildings and streets some hundred years ago. When placed next to photographs of the same scenes today the changes to the town over the past century are made very plain. Today, thanks largely to private initiative, the standard of conservation of Sandwich's historic buildings is probably higher that it has ever been, and it should be regarded as a model for other small towns with a building heritage. It is to be hoped that the standard will be maintained by generations to come.

Figure 5.5 The south side of Strand Street looking east from Number 11, The Chanter's House
(SGA PC01-207A)

Streetscapes then and now

Some drivers of large vehicles trying to negotiate Strand Street may agree with Seymour's criticism, but to the rest of us Strand Street is one of the most beautiful streets in England, not just in Sandwich. Its row of timber-framed buildings, occupying about 150m, is longer than in any other town (see Figure 4.1). They are all occupied and beautifully conserved, in great contrast to their condition in the relatively recent past, as shown in this picture of the street from Number 11 to Number 27 (Figure 5.5). Number 11 (now The Chanter's House) was a bakery, as was the house next door which carries an advertisement for Hovis bread. This part of the bakery is now called The Weavers after the hand-loom business which set up there in the first half of the 20th-century, although before that it was the Bull Inn (page 82). A very noticeable thing

about the houses in the early photographs is that almost none of them show their timbers. The fashion for stripping back to the timber frames did not really begin until the 1930s (Figure 5.6).

Figures 5.7 and 5.8 illustrate how much difference a century has made to St Peter's Street. In Figure 5.7, the first house on the left is Number 20 St Peter's Street, and the group of residents stands outside Number 18. The general air of shabbiness comes over strongly and one can almost smell the air, redolent with the horse droppings covering the thoroughfare. Compare that with Figure 5.8, which shows a beautiful row of houses (Number 18 is the one with the climbing plant beside the door) and a spick and span tarmac

street surface. We may complain that double yellow lines are aesthetically undesirable, but would we really wish to go back to a time of horse-drawn vehicles and all that that implies?

The Quay has also changed out of all recognition, from its medieval character as the commercial hub of international trade to a small port for coasters (Figure 5.9) to a destination for holidaymakers (Figure 5.10).

We could go on and on making such comparisons, but all of them would prove that the Sandwich of today is brighter, smarter, cleaner and healthier that it has ever been. During its long history it has reached the heights and plumbed the depths. From being an important mercantile and military port in the 14th and 15th centuries it became a backwater by 1600. Now it is a quiet town with an incomparable heritage of fine houses of which the residents are justly proud. It is a jewel among English towns and I hope that this book has gone some way making its beauties much better known and appreciated.

Figure 5.9 Sandwich harbour in the early 20th century, looking west from the bridge (SGA BPC00202)

Figure 5.10 The Quay at Sandwich today (GC)

Index

Numbers in bold refer to pages with figures

Books on Sandwich published since 2000

2004   Richardson, T. L., *Medieval Sandwich and its World*. Sandwich Local History Society.

2004   Richardson, T. L., *Historic Sandwich*. Sandwich Local History Society.

2005   Harris, P., *Sandwich Photographic Memories*. Black Horse Books.

2010   Clarke, H., Pearson, S., Mate, M. and Parfitt, K., *Sandwich, The 'completest medieval town in England'*. Oxbow Books.

2011   Clarke, H., *Walks through Historic Sandwich*. Oxbow Books.